JESSE JACKSON

JESSE JACKSON
THE LAST INTERVIEW
and OTHER CONVERSATIONS

with an introduction by AL SHARPTON

MELVILLE HOUSE
BROOKLYN • LONDON

JESSE JACKSON: THE LAST INTERVIEW
AND OTHER CONVERSATIONS

First Melville House Printing: October 2026

Distributed by Penguin Random House LLC, 1745 Broadway, New York, NY 10019 USA. www.penguinrandomhouse.com

Melville House Publishing
46 John Street
Brooklyn, NY 11201

and

Suite 2000
16/18 Woodford Road
London E7 0HA

mhpbooks.com
@melvillehouse

ISBN: 978-1-68589-305-7
ISBN: 978-1-68589-306-4 (EBOOK)

Printed in the United States of America
1st Printing

A catalog record for this book is available from the Library of Congress.

CONTENTS

INTRODUCTION

THE MAN WHO MADE ME BELIEVE

AL SHARPTON

There is a moment in every young person's life when they encounter someone who makes them believe that the world can be different—that they can be different—and nothing is ever the same again. For me, that moment came because of my mother.

I was twelve years old when my mother brought me to Reverend William Augustus Jones, the great pastor of Bethany Baptist Church in Brooklyn. Reverend Jones was one of the towering figures of the Black church in New York—a prophetic voice, a man of scripture and struggle. My mother saw something in me that she wanted shaped by serious men. Reverend Jones saw it too. And so, he did what serious men of God do when they recognize a spark: he passed it along. He introduced me to Reverend Jesse Louis Jackson Sr.

I was a boy. Jesse Jackson was already a force of nature.

He was young himself, by the standards of movement leadership, but he carried himself with a gravitas that seemed ancient, as if he had been forged in some furnace the rest of us hadn't yet been near. He spoke, and you did not merely hear words. You felt the architecture of history rearranging itself. I remember standing in that room thinking: This is what a leader sounds like. This is what it looks like when a man has decided, without reservation or apology, that his people's liberation is worth everything he has.

I became the youth director of Operation Breadbasket in New York not long after that. Jesse had built Operation Breadbasket as the economic arm of Dr. Martin Luther King's Southern Christian Leadership Conference (SCLC). Operation Breadbasket was a campaign to use the organized moral weight of the Black community to demand jobs, demand dignity, demand that American commerce reckon with the people it had spent centuries exploiting. As a teenager running the youth division in New York, I was learning in the most serious school I could have attended. Jesse Jackson was the professor, and the streets of America were the classroom.

What I did not fully appreciate at the time—though I came to understand it deeply as I grew older—was how much Jesse's effectiveness flowed from his formation in the Black church. He was not a politician who occasionally used religious language. He was a preacher who understood that the prophetic tradition of the Black church was itself a form of political power, perhaps the most durable political power Black Americans had ever possessed. The church had been our refuge and our launching pad, our sanctuary and our strategy room. Jesse never allowed those two realities to be separated. When he stood at a pulpit or a podium, there was no seam between the sacred and the civic. They were one fabric, and he wore it without apology and without confusion.

That integration of faith and action—that insistence that the gospel had social and economic and political consequences that you were obligated to pursue in the world—is something I carry with me every single day. Every Saturday morning at National Action Network (NAN), when the people come and we lift our voices and then we talk about the work ahead, I am drawing from a well that Jesse helped dig.

When Jesse later built Operation PUSH in Chicago, his Saturday morning rallies became something historic. A sanctuary full of people—working people, activists, clergy, young folks who needed somewhere to put their energy—coming together every week to hold power accountable and lift each other up. When I founded NAN decades later, I modeled our own Saturday morning action rallies in Harlem directly after what Jesse was doing in Chicago. I make no apologies for that. You learn from the best, and you build on what they built. That is not imitation; that is lineage. I stand in the direct line that runs from Dr. King to Jesse Jackson to the work we do at NAN today, and I have never once been embarrassed to say so. That lineage is not a burden. It is an honor.

Jesse understood that, too. When he came to Harlem and stood inside our headquarters, he looked around at what we had built—the staff, the history on those walls, the community that had grown up around that building—and he named it himself. He called it "The House of Justice." That name stayed, because that is exactly what Jesse Jackson spent his entire life trying to build: not monuments, not legacies in the self-congratulatory sense, but actual houses of justice, places where ordinary people could walk in off the street and find someone willing to fight for them.

What people sometimes forget—especially those who encountered Jesse only on television, only in the grand arena of presidential politics—is how practical he was. "Keep hope alive" was not a slogan manufactured in some consultant's office—it was a theology, a survival strategy, a direct instruction to people who had every reason to give up. Jesse meant it. He lived it.

But the preaching was always in service of the program. This is what I absorbed as a young man watching him work: that the sermon and the strategy had to be one. You could not inspire people on Sunday and leave them without a plan on Monday. Operation Breadbasket understood this. PUSH understood this. His two presidential campaigns, in 1984 and 1988, understood this. When Jesse stood before those Democratic National Conventions and spoke about the suffering of farmers in Iowa and steelworkers in Gary, Indiana, and sharecroppers in Mississippi and young Black men in Chicago in the same breath, he was not being rhetorical. He was building a coalition. He was insisting, years before it became fashionable to say so, that the poor and the working people of every color in this country had more in common with each other than with the powerful interests that pitted them against one another.

I watched him take on the Democratic establishment when it was not comfortable to do so. I watched him go to Syria in 1983 to secure the release of Lieutenant Robert Goodman—a Black naval aviator shot down over Lebanese territory—when the Reagan administration had essentially written the man off. Jesse came home with Lieutenant Goodman. He did not ask permission. He did not wait for the diplomatic machinery to grind forward at its own indifferent pace. He went, because that is who Jesse Jackson was: a man who understood that moral authority, deployed with courage, could accomplish what institutional power would not bother to attempt.

I think about that mission often. I think about what it meant to a young Al Sharpton, watching a Black preacher from Greenville, South Carolina—a man born outside of wedlock, who had known poverty and humiliation, who had been shaped by the church and by the movement and by his own relentless hunger to matter—walk into one of the most complex geopolitical situations in the world and walk back out with an American serviceman. It told me something about the power of moral seriousness. It told me that race did not have to be a ceiling. It told me that if you carried yourself with enough conviction, if your cause was righteous and your preparation thorough, you could sit at any table, walk through any door.

Jesse gave a generation of us that belief.

He is why I ran for political office. He is why I founded the National Action Network. He is why, when people told me that a Black activist from Brooklyn had no business being on a presidential debate stage in 2004, I stood there anyway.

Because Jesse had already shown me what it looked like to stand somewhere you were not invited, to refuse the limits other people set for you, and to expand what was imaginable for everyone who came behind you.

But I want to say something about the man behind the movement, because history sometimes flattens people into their greatest hits and forgets what made them human. Jesse Jackson was funny. He could read a room and find the exact line that would break the tension and bring a crowd together in laughter before he brought them back to seriousness. He was warm in private, in ways that the public Jesse—the Jesse of the podium, the Jesse of the picket line—did not always reveal. He was a man who asked after your family, who remembered details about your life that you had mentioned once in passing, who understood that relationships were the infrastructure of movements. You cannot sustain a lifetime of struggle without people around you who genuinely love you and whom you genuinely love in return. Jesse had that. He cultivated it. He knew that the long work of justice was not a solo performance but a communal vocation, and he treated the people in his circle accordingly.

I also want to say something about his resilience, because Jesse Jackson faced criticism—some of it fair, some of it wildly unfair—across every decade of his public life. He was attacked from the right for being too radical and from certain precincts of the left for not being radical enough. He was scrutinized in ways that white politicians of comparable stature were simply not scrutinized. And through all of it, he kept going. He did not retreat into bitterness. He did not allow the weight of other people's opposition to bend him away from the work. That is its own form of courage, quieter perhaps than the courage it takes to walk into a foreign capital or stand on a picket line, but no less real.

This book spans the arc of one of the most consequential careers in American public life. You will hear Jesse in many registers here: the preacher and the politician; the strategist and the dreamer; the man who ran for president twice and moved the country in the process; the elder statesman who never stopped showing up. What I hope you will take from these pages, beyond the history and the analysis, is the character of the man. The humor. The tenderness. The iron underneath the eloquence.

Jesse Jackson taught me that the measure of a leader is not the offices he holds but the doors he opens for others. By that measure, there are few in American history who stand taller.

He is gone now, and the grief is real. But so is the inheritance. And so is the obligation—the obligation to honor what he built by refusing to let it go dormant, by continuing to speak when speaking is costly, by continuing to stand in places where our presence is inconvenient to power. That is what Jesse would want from those of us he leaves behind. Not eulogies that end at the graveside, but lives that carry the work forward. Not nostalgia for what he did, but action in the spirit of why he did it.

Keep hope alive. He meant that for us. All of us.

JESSE JACKSON

"I WAS WITH DR. KING WHEN THE ASSASSIN'S BULLET WAS FIRED"

INTERVIEW BY ARTHUR KRETCHMER
PLAYBOY
NOVEMBER 1969

ARTHUR KRETCHMER: Though the mood of blacks has changed markedly since the death of Martin Luther King, are you still committed, as Dr. King was, to nonviolence as the only way to win racial justice?

JESSE JACKSON: We will be as nonviolent as we can be and as violent as we must be. We should not choose violence first, because it is an inhumane way of dealing with problems. We also do not have the military resources to deal with the American power structure. There's no sense in facing tanks with a .22 pistol. Our circumstances and terrain would not give us the freedom to use a violent strategy. The ghettos are built like a military stockade. America never needs to actually come in. The lights can be turned off, the water shut off and the food supply stopped. We could be eliminated in the ghetto without anyone even crossing the railroad tracks to get us.

KRETCHMER: Do you mean to imply that if you did have the military resources, you would wage war against white Americans?

JACKSON: I am just pointing out that there is a strong pragmatic case for nonviolence. I am philosophically committed to nonviolence because I think it is the creative alternative and should be used as long as it helps protect and sustain life. It is a creative alternative to the Pentagon, for example. Just as there are forces in this world with a design for killing, so must there be forces with a design for healing.

KRETCHMER: Stokely Carmichael and Eldridge Cleaver, among others, say that unless blacks create their own design for killing, they are going to be killed themselves. Is this an irrevocable split in the black movement?

JACKSON: No. The competition to nonviolence does not come from Stokely or Eldridge; it comes from America's traditions. It comes from little children seeing cowboys solve their moral problems by killing. The competition to nonviolence comes from the military draft, with its nine weeks' training on how to kill. The trouble is that nonviolence is so often defined as refusal to fight, and that is the American definition of cowardice. In fact, marching unarmed against the guns and dogs of the police requires more courage than does aggression. The perverted idea of manhood coming from the barrel of a gun is what keeps people from understanding nonviolence.

KRETCHMER: If your life were endangered, could you use a gun?

JACKSON: Yes. Nonviolence does not demand that one develop an absolute, universal commitment to pacifism. That old notion of being in a dark alley and having a man step out with a gun does not apply. Of course, I am going to do whatever I must to get rid of the man and his gun. I preach nonviolence because it's the better alternative. In that alley, there is no alternative. But peace is the alternative to war, and nonviolence should be seen as the antidote to violence, not simply as its opposite. Nonviolence is more concerned with saving life than with saving face. It is the most sensible way to combat white society's military oppression of blacks.

KRETCHMER: Do you think white America is actually waging war on black America?

JACKSON: Yes, it's a war. Sometimes it's waged by a white army in full military gear, as any weapons count among special riot police would show. But it's also a war of attrition, a siege, in which the violence takes other forms. To me, violence is starving a child or maintaining a mother on insufficient welfare. Violence is going to school twelve years and getting five years' worth of education. Violence is thirty million hungry in the most abundant nation on earth. White America must understand that men will steal before they starve, that if there is a choice of a man's living or dying, he will choose to live, even if it means other men die. These are human reactions, and we cannot assume that black people are going to be anything less than human.

KRETCHMER: Is there a point at which you feel violence would be justified?

JACKSON: If I saw that there was no other way for us to be liberated, yes.

KRETCHMER: For many white people, the most disturbing incident of potential black violence this year was portrayed by a news picture of armed students at Cornell. What do you think about their use of weapons?

JACKSON: They didn't use them, except in the symbolic sense of warning groups that had threatened them that they were capable of their own military defense. I have doubts about the enduring success of the technique of military defense, but I appreciate the feelings that brought such a desperate mood into existence.

KRETCHMER: Another group that has endorsed violence as a tactic is the Black Panthers, which J. Edgar Hoover has called "the greatest threat among the black extremist groups to the internal security of the United States." Do you support the Panthers?

JACKSON: I'm very sympathetic to the Panthers. They are the logical result of the white man's brutalization of blacks. The remarkable thing about them is that they have not conducted any military offenses. They have not gone to downtown America to shoot up white-owned stores. The Panthers are a defense for justice, just as the Ku Klux Klan is an offense for injustice. That's a qualitative difference between picking up a gun to keep from being brutalized and picking up a gun to inflict brutality. As far as Mr. Hoover's opinion goes, I don't think that his perspective is relevant when it comes to the problems that are facing this society—which is surprising, when you consider all the good information he gets. He certainly knows what I'm thinking about and talking about most of the time.

KRETCHMER: Does the FBI keep you under surveillance?

JACKSON: Yes. It's admitted tapping Dr. King's phone, and I used to speak with him at least twice a week. The persons he spoke with were also frequently tapped, and I don't imagine they've untapped me, as my activities have increased since his death. But anything they've heard me say, if they come around, I'll be glad to repeat out loud to them. I want to add that I consider Mr. Hoover himself to be one of the greatest threats to our national security. His wiretapping and other surveillance methods violate the principles of democracy. The FBI director doesn't account to anyone, not even to the attorney general; and, in reality, he heads what is very nearly a secret police.

It's on this subject of abusive police power that the Panthers are profound. No white community in America has a majority of black police, but black communities are militarily occupied by white police. The Panthers are right to say that the white police should be gotten out, just as the Americans were right in saying, "Get the redcoats out." We are saying, "Get the bluecoats out."

KRETCHMER: Aren't you really saying, "Get the white bluecoats out"?

JACKSON: No. We don't want white bluecoats, but we don't want black bluecoats, either. We don't want to be policed by a supreme white authority, even if the agents of the authority are black. We're saying that the black community should police itself: The authority for the police should come from the home area, not from city hall, which is alien to us, has never been sympathetic to us and openly supports the police who oppress us.

KRETCHMER: Do you think, as some radicals seem to, that America is a police state?

JACKSON: For black men, it is. Nobody in the black community who's had the experience of being made to spread-eagle over a car for no reason, or because of a simple traffic ticket, would disagree with that. Some black folks disagree, but that's because of their lack of experience. If they just keep on living, they'll confront the reality soon enough. The reality is tyranny, and the tyrant must be opposed. Whether we are called Operation Breadbasket or Black Panthers or niggers, we know who the enemy is. We will gain our freedom by being more willing to die for it than the slave master is to die to keep us enslaved.

KRETCHMER: Do you agree with the controversial Panther demand that all black prisoners be released from prison?

JACKSON: Yes, but there are probably some black men who have been so broken, whose lives have been so twisted, that they would be dangerous to all other men, both black and white, and I suppose they should not be released from confinement, though I would hope that genuine rehabilitation would replace detention. But just as the black community is a colony of white America, and those of us within that colony should be liberated, so should those of us who have been especially victimized by the viciousness of the colonial rules, and tried by the white slave master, be released. All of the black community should be liberated, and that includes those behind steel bars as well as those behind economic and social bars.

KRETCHMER: The subject of black crime preoccupies white America and, in the opinion of some commentators, helped elect Richard Nixon president. Many whites feel that their fears of black crime are completely justified, particularly in the light of your previous statement that black prisoners should be freed. How would you respond to that?

JACKSON: The Crime Commission appointed by Lyndon Johnson showed that most black crime is against blacks. The white folks who exploit us are as safe as a baby in a womb. The black man's hostility comes from the deprivation and frustration and tension of the ghetto. Most people handle that hostility surprisingly well; and those who don't, take it out on the nearest target—other blacks. Another reason black men hurt other black men is that the punishment is less than when you hurt a white man. The price for hostility against whites is too high. To talk back to a white boss is to be fired, and to make violent gestures against white people is to invite instant death. So, the hostility that is bred in the ghetto leads to suffering—but mostly by blacks, not whites.

KRETCHMER: The incidence of property crimes by blacks is very high and is increasing. Do you think the white middle class is wrong to be concerned about protecting its possessions?

JACKSON: That property usually belongs to blacks, not whites. It is the ghetto resident whose home is robbed, sometimes two or three times in the same month. Black crimes against property are the result of desperation. I said earlier that a man will steal before he starves. Black crime is crime because of need; whites commit crimes of greed. Black folks do not set up elaborate kidnappings for a million-dollar ransom. The financial value of all of the property crimes committed by blacks in one year doesn't equal the money lost in the famous salad-oil swindle. Blacks are not out for a big score; they are out to stay alive. And when he's caught, the black man can't afford bail and a good attorney. Already wounded and probably crippled by the system, he spends more time than whites inside the jail system, where he is further destroyed by it. His criminality is molded by the police state. I was especially aware of this in the South, where I grew up. The police were an absolute power; they were not merely enforcers of the law; they were the law. They could do anything they wanted, because the judges and the legal system were thoroughly racist.

KRETCHMER: Do you have any recollections of personal confrontations with the police when you were young?

JACKSON: I remember that they seemed to get a kick out of breaking down the front door if you didn't answer quickly enough. When I was a little kid, we'd run and hide under the house at the sight of a police car. Later on, they locked us up for things like vagrancy or cursing. In time, they would kill a few of the guys I grew up with, and it was always "in the line of duty." There were some humorous incidents, too. One cop in Greenville, South Carolina, became famous for locking up a black man for "reckless eyeballing"; he had been staring at a white woman about one hundred feet away. And I remember we weren't allowed to stand around the store windows while they were changing clothes on the white store dummies. My Northern friends get a big kick out of that, but it's symbolic of the awesome pattern of Southern oppression.

My own most frightening experience, though, didn't involve a policeman. There was a store on our street run by a white man named Jack. The customers were all black, and it was a comfortable place. Jack used to play with us kids all the time, and we'd run errands for him. One day, I went in and the store was full of people, but I was in a big hurry, the kind of hurry a six-year-old is always in. I said, "Jack, I'm late. Take care of me." He didn't hear me, so I whistled at him. He wheeled around and snatched a .45 pistol from a shelf with one hand and kneeled down to grab my arm in his other fist. Then he put the pistol against my head and, kneading my black arm in his white fingers, said, "Goddamn it! Don't you ever whistle at me again, you hear?" I didn't think he was really going to shoot me, even then; the thing that got to me was that none of the black people in the store did or said anything. My impression of the superpower of whites to do absolutely anything they want and get away with it right in the middle of blacks was a traumatic experience that I've never recovered from.

KRETCHMER: Are such experiences for blacks still part of the Southern heritage?

JACKSON: Yes, but less frequently, and I think Dr. King is the reason for the change. The significance of his movement can be seen only against a Southern background. He taught us that even if the police—the law—say you can't sit down, sit down anyway. In most communities until then, there weren't five men who had that kind of courage. He challenged us to stand up to the police we used to run from. In Montgomery, Alabama, the cradle of the Confederacy, he rose up and declared that black men deserve their full rights of manhood. There wasn't enough money to buy him, and there weren't enough jails to hold him. Death itself isn't enough to stop black men from being free, for crucifixion leads to resurrection.

KRETCHMER: One of the seeming ironies of the Civil Rights Movement is that while the Southern black has gone far toward winning freedom, the ghetto black in the North is in an increasingly frustrated mood. How do you explain this?

JACKSON: The Southern movement fulfilled some of the hopes it raised. We achieved our goals in the bus boycotts and the freedom rides. The public accommodation and voting-rights bills were passed. We haven't had corresponding success in the North. The Northern black has seen some progress, but his advancement doesn't compare with the advancement of white society. The economy quadruples while blacks creep along with unemployment as high as 35 and 40 percent in some black communities. When the white unemployment rate was 20 percent in 1933, it was a depression that required massive aid. But the black unemployment rate is ignored.

The most frustrated are those who have worked hardest but remain unrewarded. A black man in Chicago with a master's degree earns less than a white man with a high school diploma. You can't tell a man who has been to college that he's not educated enough to qualify for a job that goes to white high school dropouts. If you do, you castrate him. And the Northern black is more frustrated because the indifference of white colonialism in the North is more vicious than the paternalism of the South. The Northern industrialist doesn't have any emotional relationship with the black; he maintains only economic contact. In the North, you get white smiles while the shops are open, but the hypocritical charade is over when the shops close and whites take the money out of the ghetto. It's no coincidence that those stores are the primary targets in a riot.

KRETCHMER: Los Angeles mayor Sam Yorty once stated on television that he thought riots were caused by the mass media. He said that blacks rioted in imitation of the disruptive behavior they saw on television and that if there had been no television coverage of Watts during the first hours of the trouble there in 1965, there would have been no riot. Do you feel that's true?

JACKSON: That's absurd. The riots are expressions of the unheard. The rioters are the mass of black people who invest hard labor on nasty chores—they are floor cleaners, shoeshine boys, hospital attendants, and they find that they have almost no share, no investment, no dividend in a 900-billion-dollar economy. Riots are a reaction to pain and a sense of hopelessness. There are black people whom no president's program has ever reached. My grandmother has lived through every president from 1900 to 1969, and the sum total of their grassroots programs has not been able to teach her the twenty-six letters of the alphabet. Riots do not solve problems, but they indicate what those problems are. It is the responsibility of an aching man to tell the truth about his pain. It isn't to his advantage to give the appearance of happiness when he is hurting. In the past, we passively accepted the immoral acts of white society to prove that we were nice, decent folks, but that was our foolishness. Black folks assumed that Pharaoh was going to help them simply because it was the right thing to do. Now we know that Pharaoh's commitment is to property, not to persons. He must be made to do the right thing.

KRETCHMER: It has been alleged by some observers, however, that the riots reveal a kind of death wish on the part of blacks.

JACKSON: It's true that there is in the young generation an inclination toward nihilism. To challenge a police headquarters with a handful of bricks is a suicidal act, but it is also a blow for freedom. What the riots really reveal is the beastliness and sadism of white police. Nearly all of the people who died in riots were blacks killed by whites whose ethics dictate that nickels and dimes are more important than flesh and blood.

KRETCHMER: There are whites who say that activists such as yourself foster the riots, that without you, there'd be racial peace.

JACKSON: White folks don't want peace; they want quiet. The price you pay for peace is justice. Until there is justice, there will be no peace or quiet.

KRETCHMER: At the time of Dr. King's death, many blacks said that white America had lost its last chance to solve the race problem without destroying itself. Do you think that's true?

JACKSON: No, I don't, although I was one of the first people to make that statement. It seemed to me then that Dr. King's death ended America's last chance to be redeemed. But it is not for us to determine the chances of redemption. There are still people being born with hope, still people fighting with hope. God has not yet damned this country, though one may wonder how long the wicked will prosper. America at this point is the most violent nation in the world.

KRETCHMER: Isn't that a cliché? Don't other nations have wars and assassinations?

JACKSON: Of course. But no other nation wants so clearly to be the world's policeman. No other nation comes down so consistently on the wrong side of every revolutionary movement for liberation from tyranny. Wherever there is a rebellion, our conservative industrialists are helping to end it, whether it's in Angola or Venezuela. Any place we buy oil or rubber, or sell a little Coca-Cola and chewing gum, we've got to protect the old order. We spend $900 per second to kill the Vietcong but only $77 per person per year to feed the hungry at home. We maintain soldiers in twenty countries around the world, yet we always talk about the Russian threat or the Chinese threat. China does not have a standing army outside of China; Russia has two. Yet we assume that someone's after us, that the "free world" is threatened simply because people want the chance to control their own economic market so they can participate in the world decision-making order. They don't want to go Communist or to crush democracy; they just want to end their serf status, and that's all blacks want here at home.

KRETCHMER: It might seem incongruous to some that you can make this sweeping indictment of America, an indictment that could easily serve as the lead paragraph in one of SDS's [Students for a Democratic Society] revolutionary pamphlets, and yet, as economic director of SCLC [Southern Christian Leadership Conference] and leader of Operation Breadbasket, you are leading blacks who clearly want to buy into the American dream.

JACKSON: It's very simple. For all its faults, America is the only country with the capacity to save the world, even at the very moment that we seem bent on destroying it. We can produce more food, medicine, trained and educated people than anyone else. We try to export our killers, but people have stopped wanting them; they would accept our doctors, scientists and creators, but our armies are outdated. We could liberate nations from their poverty and their pestilence if our value system would allow us to do so. The irony is how close we are to being something great. One-fifth of our nation is starving, yet we have the capacity to overfeed it. We could end the starvation in India, heal the sickness in Africa. But the tragedy is that we are as close to destroying the world as we are to saving it. We spent 78.4 billion dollars to kill this year but only 12 billion to heal. Those who are silent now, or are neutral now, must make a decision before the opportunity passes forever.

KRETCHMER: Are you encouraged by the young white radicals who seem determined to change America's value system?

JACKSON: The issues that move them are qualitatively different from the ones that concern blacks. Many of the radical whites say that materialism is no good, that one must seek a new level of spiritualism. Well, we lived for years with spiritualism but without any materialism. Now we'd like to try to balance the two. Many of the young whites are living on the prerogatives of the materialism they shun. They confront their school in the winter, but in the summer, they go off to Sweden or Hawaii. Their discussions of America's corruption take place over steaks. They spend $5,000 a year to attend the schools they shut down. We often have the same moral ideals, but the perspective is very different.

I have also been disappointed that we were unable to get any mass help from young whites on the hunger caravan we recently concluded in Illinois. The students were so radical that feeding starving people didn't constitute revolution to them, because "a man needs to do more than eat." But while they were saying that, they were eating very well. To us, they tend to be superfluous.

KRETCHMER: Weren't the strikes at both Harvard and Columbia concerned mainly with accusations by white students that those schools abuse the black community?

JACKSON: I do not mean to condemn their creative protests. They accurately reflect Jesus's position that man cannot live by bread alone. They come from houses with boats and cars and more money than they can spend, yet they find their lives empty. There is beauty in their hearing the heartbeats of other humans. What I'm saying is that there is a lack of depth in their protest, in terms of the black community's real and immediate needs. But I think I must reserve judgment on those whites who are living off the prerogatives of wealth. If they are legitimately concerned, they will take what Daddy leaves and pay back some of that money in reparations to blacks.

KRETCHMER: Do you agree with James Forman's proposal that the churches pay reparations to blacks?

JACKSON: Yes, and eventually the demands will not be limited to the churches. The black community in America is an underdeveloped nation, a victim of America's cold war against her own black people. In that war, all of our supply lines have been cut—educational, commercial, political and psychological. We've been the victims of an unjust war and are due reparations from those who launched it. Business owes us reparations, first for enslaving us, then for refusing to give us work or hiring us for only the lowest paying, most grueling jobs. And even when we have an opportunity to do the same work as white men, we are paid less for it. The labor unions, for whom we fought, owe us reparations for locking us out. The church is also liable, because it has disregarded its own moral imperatives and cooperated in creating and maintaining a racist society.

KRETCHMER: Do you expect these demands to be met?

JACKSON: For the most part, no.

KRETCHMER: Then isn't the plea for reparations a rhetorical gesture rather than a serious proposal?

JACKSON: The demands are perfectly serious. If they were met, it would mean a great step toward unifying the two separate and unequal societies that the Kerner Commission described after it studied the Newark and Detroit riots. The point is that SCLC and I are not naïve enough to think that the businessmen who control the assets of corporations, labor unions and churches will voluntarily act from some inner moral impetus. America's god is money. God is your ultimate concern, what you give maximum sacrifice for, what you will die for. God is what you worship. The American ideal is maximum profit and minimum person; there is no impulse to share the wealth, to raise up those less fortunate. What counts is the name on the front of the building. Well, I say what counts are the hands that do the work inside.

KRETCHMER: Isn't money also one of Operation Breadbasket's major concerns?

JACKSON: Yes. It's a concern because it's a reality. But the essential purpose of Operation Breadbasket is to have blacks control the basic resources of their community. We want to control the banks, the trades, the building construction and the education of our children. This desire on our part is a defensive strategy evolved in order to stop whites from controlling our community and removing the profits and income that belong to black people. Our programs are dictated by the private enterprise economy in which we find ourselves. In my heart, however, I know that the entire system is a corruption. To me, the earth belongs to everybody; it's just a very successful rumor white folks have going that the earth belongs to them. The earth is the Lord's and no man creates anything that didn't come from other things that God put here. No man really takes anything away, either. No man can claim that he made soil or wool or milk. White folks can make airplanes, but they can't make mountains. They can make syrup but not water. Genesis says that the Lord created the earth and everything therein and gave man, not white man, dominion over it and created a dominion sufficient for everyone to be able to survive and prosper. Now the concept of Genesis has obviously been destroyed, and it is our concern to rid America of some of her arrogance and control of God's resources by saying that the food belongs to all the people.

KRETCHMER: Do you think farmers and suppliers should give their food away?

JACKSON: I don't care how the people get food, as long as they get it. The Government can buy the food and give it away in a large-scale version of the present inadequate surplus-food and food stamp programs. Or it can give the poor enough money to buy the food themselves.

KRETCHMER: Many middle-class whites think that the poor would only buy booze and guns if they had the money.

JACKSON: I challenge anyone with that belief to tour the reeking, rat-infested tenements of Harlem or Chicago's South Side and count the number of alcoholic welfare mothers. There won't be many. Welfare people do not account for this nation's high number of alcoholics. Nor are most guns bought by the black poor. In a home where the children are eating wall plaster because they are hungry, a gun isn't looked upon as an important commodity. But I don't care if the Government wants to give out food instead of money. I would bless any device it might come up with, as long as it does something. The country is producing more food than it needs. There is inherent evil in a system that induces men to plow crops under while others starve.

Not only does the food belong to the people but the industrial profit also belongs to the people. If the employees of General Motors [GM] left tomorrow, it would have to stop. If the entire board of directors died tomorrow, nothing would stop. What's indispensable are the laborers, not the directors. The laborers can rise from the ranks and direct their fellow laborers. Because they are the basic need, they ought to reap the basic benefits. But in America, about 6 percent of the people control the basic wealth, and there's something infinitely demonic about that. It's no wonder that America needs the largest military in the world to protect the wealthiest superrich class from people who would rebel against it. There's no basic conflict among the peoples of the world; Russian bus drivers aren't mad at American bus drivers. But the controlling groups are always in conflict with the people—whether it's the Government of the United States, which refuses to adequately protect the poor, or the boards of directors at GM and Ford, which encourage blacks to go into debt to buy automobiles but don't allow blacks to participate in the profitable manufacture and distribution of cars.

KRETCHMER: Can blacks afford to buy automobile agencies?

JACKSON: The companies will lend us the money to buy cars, which leads to profits for them only. They could lend us the money to buy agencies, but they won't, because that would let us profit also.

KRETCHMER: Aren't there some black car dealers?

JACKSON: About fourteen dealerships out of twenty-eight thousand. We are grossly underrepresented in all areas of the economy. There are no black TV stations, for example, and only seven black radio stations. Most of the stations that are beamed toward the black community and play black music are white owned. We can't get FCC [Federal Communications Commission] outlets, and I'm convinced that there is a conspiracy to keep us from communicating with one another on a mass scale.

KRETCHMER: Do you mean that the Government fears a nationally directed riot?

JACKSON: I don't know what they think; all I know is we can't get licenses when we apply.

KRETCHMER: What does Operation Breadbasket intend to do about this sort of economic underrepresentation?

JACKSON: We have the power, nonviolently, just by controlling our appetites, to determine the direction of the American economy. If black people in thirty cities said simultaneously, "General Motors, you will not sell cars in the black community unless you guarantee us a franchise here next year and help us finance it," GM would have no choice. We can affect their margin of profit by withdrawing our patronage and resisting the system instead of enduring it.

KRETCHMER: Can this really work? And, if so, why hasn't it been done already?

JACKSON: It hasn't been done because we weren't sophisticated enough to see it. This is a step that we haven't been ready to take. But it will certainly be done now, because we are organizing to do it. Black people purchase about 35 to 40 billion dollars' worth of goods each year. We represent the margin of profit in many industries. America depends on our cooperation with her economy, and we shall become the enemies of those businesses and industries that work against our interest by unfair hiring practices, by discriminating against black products, by not making investments in the ghetto to correspond with the profits taken out of it. There is an analogous situation in politics: The black people have not yet realized that we can determine who gets elected president; in 1960, it was the South Side of Chicago that turned in the vote that made John Kennedy president. The newspapers all said that Mayor Daley had once again come through with his Cook County machine, but that vote was black. The ghetto, however, has seldom voted in its own self-interest. It has even voted for black politicians who are contemptuous of blacks.

KRETCHMER: Why does the ghetto vote so inefficiently?

JACKSON: Because it's so easy to intimidate or con the poor; they have no recourse. On Election Day, the precinct worker comes around and says that if you don't vote his way, he'll have you thrown out of the housing project or he'll have your welfare check canceled. Or, if he's a benign type, he'll buy your vote with a chicken. The poor are also frightened out of coming to freedom meetings. But the poor themselves must learn that food is a right and not a privilege. We are marching to gain a subsidy for thirty million hungry Americans who represent a human resource that is more important than any of the mineral resources that this nation subsidizes.

KRETCHMER: What form would that subsidy take?

JACKSON: A guaranteed annual income based upon the Government's own estimate of the amount of money people actually need to live adequate lives. They say that a family of four in a large city in the United States in 1969 requires $5,994 per year for minimum maintenance. If that's what's needed, then that's what they should get.

KRETCHMER: Wouldn't that be expensive. especially considering the present high tax burden?

JACKSON: The Senate committee on poverty headed by George McGovern stated, after doing field research throughout the nation, that it would cost 10 billion dollars per year to feed the poor and fulfill their basic health, clothing and housing needs. I would guess that that's a low estimate. Let's double it and say that the cost would be 20 billion dollars per year. That's less money than we're spending to kill the Vietcong. It's less money than we're about to spend on the ABM [Anti-Ballistic Missile] system. It is less than a third of the defense budget. If we wanted men to live as much as we want to see them die, we could do it without any new taxes.

KRETCHMER: But what motivation does the Government have to subsidize the poor?

JACKSON: Out of a spirit of humanity, one would hope; but that is naïve. Our job is to create enough pressure to force the Government to act. It is certainly not going to do so on its own. The imbalance of Southern power in the Congress has led to important committees being headed by pathological killers and by men with public commitments to racism. These men—such as Mendel Rivers, Russell Long, Jamie Whitten and Richard Russell—are the black man's burden. The truth is that the Mafia is probably better represented in the Government than blacks are. And numerous other special-interest groups are well taken care of. The situation on the agriculture committees is particularly loathsome to me because of the millions of dollars that are given away to gentleman farmers who don't farm, while children are starving. Contrast that with the Black Panthers' national breakfast program. They are serving thousands of people free food every week, and the only qualification is that the recipient be hungry. If the Panthers can serve breakfast to 3000 children a week in Chicago or 1500 in San Francisco, with their lack of resources, what could those cities' governments be doing if they had the same interest?

KRETCHMER: If you were the mayor of a major American city, what would you do?

JACKSON: I would declare the poor communities in a state of emergency and deal with the unemployment rate, the high mortality rate and the high TB [tuberculosis] rate. I would set up medicine tents on the streets, and embarrass the federal and state governments into opening up their food storehouses. I would declare war on disease and hunger. I would enlarge all the city departments that feed and heal people. The welfare of all the people would be attended to before any new golf courses or monuments or stadiums were built. I would force the Government to call out the National Guard to deal with the existing injustices, which make the ghetto a permanent disaster area. There's no reason why the army couldn't be coming down the street with bayonets, looking for slum landlords. The army would force trade unions to allow the minority groups in. And those who did not pick up the garbage would themselves be picked up. An army like that wouldn't have any trouble getting volunteer soldiers because it would be engaged in a relevant war.

KRETCHMER: Is that statement a reference to Vietnam?

JACKSON: Let me just say that Vietnam is not a relevant war. It is a war in which the black poor are paying with their lives to protect the investments of a small, rich elite whose Asian investments are threatened by Hanoi.

KRETCHMER: Whatever interests are being served in Vietnam, do you think that you, as a citizen, have the right to pick the wars in which you will fight and those in which you won't?

JACKSON: Of course I have that right. I must reserve the right to decide which wars are just. And I would not fight in a war that I thought was unjust. Nor would I approve of anyone else doing so.

KRETCHMER: Would you encourage drafted blacks to refuse to go to Vietnam, even if it means jail for them?

JACKSON: Yes. And whites, too. Fighting in Vietnam is a step back into slavery for blacks, and into barbarism for whites. The road to jail has often been the road to freedom. Many men—Gandhi, Jomo Kenyatta, Dr. King—have learned that.

KRETCHMER: Although a disproportionate number of blacks have died in Vietnam, there have been few blacks active in the peace movement. Why?

JACKSON: To blacks, the peace movement is a luxury that presupposes you have the time to save somebody aside from yourself. Blacks are just too occupied with their own survival. They have not even been sophisticated enough to know that they can oppose murder. A black man can be easily seduced; it's a revolution for him to go from one meal a day to three. Sometimes I think that blacks are so locked away from information that we could be duped into fighting in South Africa for apartheid, if America told us to do it. We certainly were down there shooting our Dominican brothers. I saw televised scenes of Dominicans lined up against a wall while black GIs held guns on them. But this is not because of ignorance but because of cultural suffocation and improper education.

KRETCHMER: Malcolm X once proposed that the UN [United Nations] send observers into the American black community to determine if blacks were being treated humanely. Do you think that's a practical idea?

JACKSON: Only for symbolic purposes; the UN doesn't have any power and is subject to the American veto.

KRETCHMER: Wouldn't exercising the veto prove so embarrassing to the U.S. that it would refrain from doing so?

JACKSON: I doubt it. And the countries that one might expect to pressure America into dealing humanely with its black minority—the countries of Africa—are themselves too dependent on America's trade and financial aid to wish to antagonize her. It is not in the enlightened self-interest of those countries to rise up in indignation when we're shot up in Detroit or Watts, because we don't affect their essential relationship with the world markets or the World Bank.

KRETCHMER: Both Malcolm and Dr. King worked to mobilize a worldwide conscience against racism before they were struck down. Do you share the view of some that both murders were part of a plan to deprive blacks of their leaders?

JACKSON: Not a single elaborate conspiracy, but it's clear that as we have moved closer to America's nerve center, closer to a position where we could vote men out of office, the killings have increased. And I don't think America has done anything to indicate that she is on the side of Dr. King rather than of his killers.

KRETCHMER: You used the plural. Don't you think that James Earl Ray acted alone?

JACKSON: I would be surprised if it wasn't a conspiracy involving many others.

KRETCHMER: Do you have any evidence to support that belief?

JACKSON: I think the circumstances were very suspicious. As you know, I was with Dr. King when the assassin's bullet was fired. We were talking with Operation Breadbasket's music director, Ben Branch, about songs for the next day's rally. Dr. Abernathy, Andy Young, James Bevel and Bernard Lee were very near. When Dr. King was shot, I hit the ground, along with the others. We scrambled toward the steps where he was and I looked back over my shoulder, because I was afraid that more shots were going to be fired. I saw so many police coming from the direction of the shot that I actually threw up my hands, thinking that the shot had come from one of them and that I was going to be killed, too. There were hundreds of police in the area, some jumping from the hill where the shot had come from. I tried to tell them that the bullet came from that way.

Now, the hotel that Ray was in—if Ray was the killer—is next door to the fire department. With the shot having been fired and all those police in the area, the usual thing during an emergency in a Southern town would be for a siren to go off that stops the lights and traffic on Main Street, where the hotel is. It was six o'clock in the afternoon, the busiest time for traffic, and it all could have been brought to a halt. But no siren went off, traffic wasn't stopped and Ray escaped through downtown Memphis. The distance he subsequently traveled indicates to me that he didn't do it by himself and that he may have had some very highly placed help. But, of course, finding Dr. King's killers is secondary to getting at the roots of America's violent atmosphere—an atmosphere in which you conform or are broken, in which you take your subordinate place in the industrial hierarchy or are destroyed.

KRETCHMER: What do you think Dr. King would be doing if he were alive today?

JACKSON: Dr. King would still be dealing with the problem of finding a job for everybody; he would still be raising the questions of medical care for everybody, of a full-employment economy. He would still be on the basic issues, still be pointing out the stupidity of the war. He would be in general conflict with Nixon. He would still, as we say, be on the case.

KRETCHMER: Will there ever be another black leader as important as Dr. King?

JACKSON: I don't think so, though, of course, no man can say. But it was Dr. King who crossed the frontier, who made a permanent break with the past. I grew up in the period from 1955 to 1965, and that time was dominated by his courage and strength, as opposed to the previous mass docility of black men. Dr. King was a surprise for a lot of whites who had conned themselves into believing that Negroes were really inferior. He was intelligent, moral, eloquent and courageous. The contrast of his eloquence with the lack of it in those whites he was forced to deal with gave us a rallying point. Even more important was the way he stood up to white military power in the South. Dr. King wasn't afraid of the cop's billy stick, guns or dogs. He overcame the stigma of jail cells; in fact, he dignified the jail cell and wrote great words from it. He was willing to die for black people, and finally did die, not on some lofty mountainside or in the company of ambassadors but kissing garbagemen, trying to set them free.

KRETCHMER: In the weeks before he died, did Dr. King express any particular optimism or pessimism about the future of the movement?

JACKSON: He expressed both. SCLC was at that time involved in making its decision about the Poor People's Campaign in Washington, D.C., that ultimately led to Resurrection City. Many of Dr. King's friends and some board members said that we should not go to Washington because of the possibility of a riot. The final decision was his. He was going through a bad time and he showed it at one of the last staff meetings he would ever attend. He was despairing that morning, and Andy Young tried to tell him to relax, that things were going to get better. And Dr. King told Andy, "Don't say 'Peace, peace' when there is no peace. The country is swinging to the right and our president is obsessed with the war. Maybe I ought to turn around," he said. But then he stopped; and when he continued, his voice was more firm. "But we've gone too far to turn around. There were dark days during the sit-ins, and in Selma and Birmingham. We've come too far."

Then he changed again. "But I'm still disturbed by the division in the country. Maybe I ought to just fast. And when I get to the point of death, perhaps we could have a summit meeting of blacks. Maybe that would bring us together." But then he seemed to resolve the argument in his mind. He said, "I've seen where we've got to go. We are going to fight the good fight; we are going to liberate our brothers and raise up the poor. We're not going to turn around. It's all very clear to me now." And I think Dr. King at that moment was as sure as he had ever been of the ultimate victory of his movement. Once you've been to the mountaintop, it doesn't matter if James Earl Ray is in the bushes waiting for you.

KRETCHMER: Do you share Dr. King's vision?

JACKSON: In my stronger moments. I have no doubts. I'm even able to love those who persecute me. There must be some force that's committed to redemption, even though it's painful. The alternative is that we will destroy ourselves, "die together as fools," as Dr. King said once. He and Gandhi and Jesus reached a spiritual state that liberates the self. Dr. King did not represent ordinary men. That's what made people love him so much. But what finally happens to the extraordinary men is what happened to Jesus. We admire them but we don't follow them, and finally we kill them because they become such a threat to us.

KRETCHMER: In what way?

JACKSON: Most of us cannot live up to the ideal of the noble and virtuous. Such men make us aware that we must settle for the real and the expedient. We are diminished by their purity, which is a threat to our self-esteem. The idealist keeps our consciences awake, but the pressure on our conscience is so great that it can be relieved only by murder.

KRETCHMER: Dr. King was criticized for placing too much emphasis on conscience. David Halberstam wrote that Dr. King left Chicago in 1966, for example, because he could not inspire a moral consciousness, and Mayor Daley was able to dissipate his campaign with high-sounding but unspecific resolutions. Do you think that Dr. King was too concerned with the moral rather than the tactical aspects of the Civil Rights Movement?

JACKSON: No, I think that even as recently as 1966, Dr. King was correctly analyzing his problem as the need to change the psyche of the black man. You couldn't impress black folks unless you impressed white folks first. Dr. King had to make the movement as large as possible in white eyes to get respect for blacks. I think that we are inclined to lose perspective on how much things have changed since 1955. There was no black consciousness then. Dr. King was dealing with "Negroes"—put quotes around that—whose minds, desires, ambitions and images were white inspired. Aretha Franklin couldn't have made it in 1955. It was Dr. King who moved the "Negro" farther and farther out; and the farther he got from that white shore, the blacker he became.

Dr. King had the most national influence of any black leader, and his concern was to change national policy. The strategy was always to form a coalition of conscience between the black community and a segment of the white community. An issue had to be defined along moral lines, because the white community will split on the basis of moral against immoral, liberal against conservative. Without that white help, there is no chance for us to have an impact on national policies. Dr. King used to point out that there is not a black college in the country that could remain open six months on black contributions. That's a reality we must face. Even now, there is no civil rights organization of any consequence that functions on black money.

KRETCHMER: Does Operation Breadbasket accept white money?

JACKSON: SCLC accepts any money, and it finances us. But we get more black money out of Chicago than any other civil rights organization has ever gotten out of the black community.

KRETCHMER: What does SCLC think of white participation in the leadership of Breadbasket and other programs?

JACKSON: We discourage it. We need and want to encourage the technical and financial aid of whites in the Civil Rights

Movement, but we should make our own decisions. Whites should spend their physical energy liberating white America, because white folks need someone to help them understand blacks or they're going to continue to be paralyzed by their paranoia. Whites suffer from nightmares and irrational anxiety. When a black family moves onto a white street, the white girls are not magically impregnated by a black boy. Those fears are unreal. But whites do not allow enough communication with blacks to learn the truth. So other white folks must defend our humanity, even though our skin color is different and our hair grows differently and we have a different heritage.

KRETCHMER: Why is there a preoccupation now with black studies and Afro styles?

JACKSON: The so-called natural movement is simply trying to say that I may not know who I am psychologically and historically, but I'm not going to be defined by white folks any longer. I want to see how I'd look if I just grew. If I didn't use anything white folks gave me to fancy myself up with, what would I look like? Most of us have never given ourselves a chance to find out. We're in search of our existence as a new people—Afro-American. White people forced us to suppress our beauty; now we want to glorify it. The fact that our natural selves conflict with the comfortable, stereotyped white image of the black man is not our problem.

KRETCHMER: But this new emphasis on blackness seems to lead to some paradoxical situations. In spite of the need for expanded opportunities for blacks to attend college, a number of strikes were initiated last year by black college students who demanded black-studies programs at their schools. Are black-studies programs so important that it's worth closing down a school to get them?

JACKSON: I think so. History plays a large role in a people's growth. The white man took away our history because it was one more way for him to control us. Without a group identity, we had no group loyalty; we were separated from our past to make it easier to control us in the present. It is one thing to see ourselves as a people only three hundred years old, born as slaves and moving toward freedom. But, in fact, our forebears date back to the origin of man, and we have always been a creative and productive people; we were enslaved, but now we are returning to freedom—and it's good to come back home. We need the pride and dignity of knowing that we are part of a great continuum. Anthropologists say that mankind originated in Africa. We are the people who carved out the great civilizations of Kush, Songhai, Ghana and Mali. We smelted iron; we mined copper and gold. For us to know this is to know that we can look forward to a great destiny.

KRETCHMER: It's the idea of exclusively black studies that bothers many white people. Other ethnic groups don't have special study programs, do they?

JACKSON: But they do, and the schools recognize them as such. If you are an Italian, for instance, your history courses will cover the entire history of early Rome and then

Renaissance Italy, and they will stress the worth of the Italian contributions. But no ancient-history courses emphasize the blackness of the great early civilizations. And American-history courses generally ignore the black man. If the schools had done their job, they wouldn't have the problems they are now confronted with—and richly deserve.

KRETCHMER: Many athletes and entertainers—Bill Cosby, for example—have adopted Afro hair and clothing styles; but aside from this sort of symbolic identification, do you think successful blacks have been as involved as they should be with the movement?

JACKSON: I think the symbolism is important; it shows a new sensitivity. The black athletes and entertainers who are wearing natural hairstyles and Afro clothes are specifically defying the white measurement apparatus. But the fact is that the black artist has never been as far away from the black community as the white press sometimes portrays him. Every black man, for example, knows where Sammy Davis's heart is. The black entertainer moves into a white community because the houses are bigger and better there. He is just taking advantage of a new freedom. Historically, the black athlete and entertainer have been in a precarious position where, if they overidentified with the racial situation, they couldn't play in the major nightclubs, couldn't get into a movie or were blackballed from a league. Black athletes who take a militant position on the race problem endanger their jobs, even though teams are dependent on their participation. Jackie Robinson broke into baseball in 1945. In 1969, blacks dominate the game. The stars of the National Basketball Association are nearly all black, as are many in the National Football League. But we'd be doing even better in sports if there were not still some discrimination there.

KRETCHMER: What kind of discrimination?

JACKSON: Before I entered college, I was offered a contract to pitch for the Chicago White Sox. They wanted to give me less money to sign than the white boys I was striking out. I'm sure that's generally true, and many black boys can't afford to leave the farm or the factory to try to make it with a team. More indicative of the racism still alive in sports is the fact that in all of major-league baseball, there isn't one black executive or manager.

KRETCHMER: If a black baseball player clearly shows himself to be managerial material, don't you think he'll get a shot at a manager's job?

JACKSON: What does that mean? Is every white manager "managerial material"? Then how come they're always being fired? In America, a white man, no matter how dumb, is expected to boss a black man; but no black man, no matter how highly qualified, is allowed to give orders to a white man. If a white ballplayer like Eddie Stanky is argumentative and aggressive, he's considered fiery. Therefore, he's a managerial prospect.

But Jackie Robinson was fiery as hell, only they called it arrogance. He was an "uppity nigger." When Robinson left baseball, his accumulated knowledge about running bases, pitching, hitting and fielding went with him. It was a waste of a great baseball mind.

KRETCHMER: You seem to be saying that unless a black man is docile, he can't survive; yet the mood of young blacks—including you—is anything but docile. Haven't the times changed?

JACKSON: We have changed; I don't know about the times. White society still tries to impose a different code of behavior on blacks than on whites. What to me is an expression of confidence is to white folks an expression of defiance. The country is so used to black people smiling and bowing and acting unsure of themselves that when whites meet someone who confronts them and challenges their standards, they make harsh judgments. Now things are changing so fast that the hostility of white society toward a black man may lead to respect for him from the black community. For a white man to embrace you is for a black man to hold you suspect.

KRETCHMER: You have been accused of cynically manipulating that new mood in your personal choice of dress and hairstyle. Do you think that if you didn't wear sideburns and a dashiki, but dressed conservatively and looked somewhat like a young Martin Luther King, that you could make it as a black leader today?

JACKSON: Style—whether it's Afro or Ivy League—isn't crucial. Hell, there are kids around who look like Che

Guevara, but they still need their mommas to get them across the street. Because of all the losses we have suffered, black people are looking for winners; that's the only way to get their respect. And a winner is someone who successfully defies white America. The reason Joe Louis will always be respected in the black community is that at a time when other blacks couldn't even talk back to white people, Joe Louis was beating them up, knocking them down and making them bleed.

When I do a TV show, I'm aware that every black watching is scoring me against the white opposition, as if I were in a fight. Every black man who has won the loyalty of his community has indicated some expression of defiance for the white man. Malcolm X is a good example. He could look Whitey straight in the eye and tell him he was lying. And Malcolm showed that even the most brutalized experience could be overcome.

KRETCHMER: You obviously don't agree with those who felt that Malcolm was a disruptive force.

JACKSON: Malcolm had become an apostle of peace after his trips to the Near East. America has a knack for killing her men of peace, while men of war continue to thrive. Malcolm's death also pointed up the futility of thinking in exclusively white-black terms. Blacks killed Malcolm, just as a black man betrayed Marcus Garvey and a black woman once tried to stab Dr. King. Black is not always good, just as white is not always bad. We confirmed that lesson at Resurrection City, where white Appalachians shared the mud with us while some blacks on U Street were asking The Man to run us out of town. And it was a black woman who started many of Adam Powell's troubles.

KRETCHMER: The consensus among white liberals is that Adam Powell deserved his fate—and that he was a hindrance to the Civil Rights Movement. Do you disagree?

JACKSON: Absolutely. First of all, and to set the record straight, as head of the House education and labor committee, Adam Powell was responsible for passing over sixty pieces of significant social legislation—more than any other of his virtuous colleagues have ever done. But Adam is even more important, for a depressed black psyche, as a defier of white rules. Something happened to my dad in World War II that illustrates this. He was serving in France and Strom Thurmond came to speak to his all-black regiment. The senator's message was that they were there to fight the war, that they were not to bother any women; they were to know their place. In other words, it was all right for my father to risk his life to serve America, but he was still a nigger. So, when Adam Powell walked down the halls of Congress with two white women on his arm, just the outrageous defiance of it gave us gratification. The appeal of that defiance will never be lost.

KRETCHMER: That story touches on the strong sexual aspect of racism. Both Malcolm X and Eldridge Cleaver have expressed elaborate theories in which white sexual fears are cited as a fundamental cause of race hatred. Do you agree?

JACKSON: Although sex is a crucial underlying cause of prejudice and racial hatred, it is not relevant to the black liberation movement. We will not allow the white man's sexual problem to stand in the way of our freedom.

KRETCHMER: Can you just ignore it?

JACKSON: Let me explain it with some awful history. In the South, when a slave ran away—thereby expressing his manhood and independence—and he was caught, the punishment for his first offense was whipping or branding. If he ran away again, which was the clearest way for him to assert himself, his punishment was likely to be castration. The slave was told that he was inferior, less than human and completely unappealing to the white woman; but The Man still castrated him. That says a lot about the psychosexual dilemma of the Southern white male. The other part of that dilemma was that because of his fear of black men, the white man had to desensitize white women. The white woman had to spiritually kill herself. For a white woman to see Jim Brown and not think of him as an attractive male means that the nerves are dead within her being. She dehumanized herself, because white men wanted it that way. But when the white man destroyed his relationship with his women, he got his satisfaction from the pursuit of money. So the white man perverted himself and his women.

If some great psychoanalyst had emerged three hundred years ago, he might have solved some of the white man's problems and prevented the brutalization of blacks by whites. But we were not rescued, and the intervening three hundred years have served to diminish the importance of sexual antagonisms and replace them with a more crippling form of racism. Today, racism is integrated into the ideology of capitalism. I said that the sexual aspect is irrelevant because even if sexual tensions disappeared tomorrow, capitalism would still require a racist ideology in order to maintain a cheap labor base. Racism provides a mechanism by which the slave master assures that society will have a ready supply of inferiors who can serve as slaves. Racism is as important to America's domestic colonialism as it was to foreign colonialism; it is an excuse to exploit and enslave a people because they have been defined as inferior. Colonialism is not built upon emotions; it is built upon behavior patterns that are designed to get a profit.

KRETCHMER: Do you think, as some revolutionaries do, that capitalism will have to be destroyed in order to end racism?

JACKSON: It is futile for us to think about ending racism; that is a psychological problem that seems beyond our attempts to affect it. We are fighting to end colonialism—oppression and exploitation. That requires power. The Civil Rights Movement is a lifetime struggle for power. A man who is impotent, no matter how courteous and pleasant looking he is, is told to wait in the lobby. But if you have power, you can be an illiterate boor with tobacco juice running down your face and they will open the door for you. As I said earlier, we are going to organize to exert power on the big corporations. We are going to see to it that the resources of the ghetto are not siphoned off by outside groups. Right now, black exterminating companies don't even get the contracts to kill the ghetto's rats. But that's going to change. If a building goes up in the black community, we're going to build it. And we're going to stop anyone else from building it. If we can't get into those construction unions, they're not going to get into our neighborhoods.

KRETCHMER: But other neighborhoods don't control their business according to ethnic separation. They try to become part of what is traditionally called the American melting pot.

JACKSON: I hear that melting-pot stuff a lot, and all I can say is that we haven't been melted. We've been getting burned on the bottom of the pot. We don't want anything that's different from the experience of the other ethnic groups. If you go into an Irish neighborhood, most of the businesses are run by Irishmen. The same is true in a Chinese or Jewish or Italian neighborhood. The difference between all of them and us is that they are all separate and independent groups, while we are separate and dependent. We want to control the vital elements of our lives: the school boards, the churches, the businesses, the police. The other groups are separate and control themselves, but they are separate and control us as well. That is a colonial situation. And the slums will exist as long as the colonists continue to turn a profit on them. As in any other revolution, we must fight for our independence.

KRETCHMER: But Dr. King once said that his aim was to "break open the city," so that ultimately there would be no separate black and white communities. Have you forsaken that goal?

JACKSON: No. But we recognize that a major part of the black community must first gravitate around itself, as other ethnic groups have done. In these areas, where our living together provides collective security, we ought to have the right to control it. But just as we have the private right to stay where we choose, we should also have the public right to participate in the public arena the way other people do. A man should choose where he wants to live, based on his income, or the fact that a house is close to his job, or because there's a good school nearby; he should not be refused because of his color. He should not be afraid of being bombed out by white bigots or of being harassed by police when he returns from work.

KRETCHMER: Aren't the open-housing laws changing this?

JACKSON: No. There is still segregation. In Chicago, blacks are 30 percent of the population, but they live on 10 percent of the land. That congestion is inhuman and a prime target for exploitation by slumlords. People are cramped in body and spirit, and those who can't afford it are paying more for the space in which they live. We are locked away from the resources of the community. Black children who are sick are untended and left to play in their own filth in understaffed, ill-equipped hospitals. Four- and five-year-olds who were lucky enough to enter Head Start programs substantially raised their learning capacity, only to have it fall again as soon as they entered public school. Yet the teachers call the children incompetent. We have no choice about schools and hospitals, because public mobility is denied us. When a white mother decides to move because her neighborhood doesn't serve the needs of her children, the broker asks her where she would like to live; when a black mother faces that problem, she knows where she can live—and where she can't.

In white communities, there are about three thousand people per square mile; in the ghetto, there are thirty thousand people in each square mile. The overcrowding produces bent and perverted people. They are made to suffer so much pain that they feel no need to conserve themselves or their neighborhoods, so they decide to destroy. These are the unheard—until they riot.

KRETCHMER: The majority of those who have participated in riots are in their teens or early twenties. Why?

JACKSON: These kids have an awful lot of reasons for hating America. Their experiences with the dominant culture are nearly all negative; whether it be in school or a courtroom or applying for a job, they are being either deprived or discriminated against. This sense of resentment is acute, and it's just a matter of time before they give up on themselves and this country. Many of them already have. If Richard Nixon really cared about America's future, he'd be showing up at Operation Breadbasket meetings and offering to join us in the fight to reclaim these kids' minds and souls, because they are going to have a large effect on that future. He might at least give us equal time and attention with the moon shot.

KRETCHMER: Weren't you impressed by the moon landing as a scientific achievement?

JACKSON: The only thing that moon shot did for me was turn my stomach. I was in a migrant worker's shack in Georgia a few weeks before the launch. It was about 115 degrees inside in the daytime. It had no toilet—not even an outhouse. No refrigerator, no running water. There was greasy butcher's paper over the space where there should have been windows. The shack was temporary residence for a family of four and they actually paid rent for it. If they hadn't rented it, they wouldn't have been allowed to work the harvest. They were all hungry. The kids' bodies were bloated and discolored. And they suffered from worms. This was [a] good time for these people. When the harvest ends, they have to move on and they have nowhere to go. That Sunday night of the moon walk, in my mind's eye, I could see those poor, broken people walking four miles to the company store to watch the two astronauts jump around. Each step Armstrong took cost enough money to feed that family for one hundred years.

America has spent 57 billion dollars since 1957 for the ego gratification of planting her flag on top of everyone else. One-tenth of that was spent in the same period to inadequately feed the hungry. The psychological state of this nation is revealed by the fact that the men whose egos are swelled by putting a flag on a dead rock would not feel the slightest sense of accomplishment from the more humane task of feeding hungry people.

KRETCHMER: Are you encouraged by Nixon's proposals about black capitalism?

JACKSON: Not very much. It is a limited vision to make a few people rich, whereas SCLC's Poor People's Campaign proposes a decent economic base for all people. Dr. King died talking about raising the level of dignity for all men. The difference between Dr. King and Mr. Nixon is the difference between a prophet and a politician. I don't believe the Government has plans for the extensive development of the black community. If it did, then the Job Corps would not have been curtailed recently. Even more serious is the Government's lack of understanding of the problems of the potential black businessman and its failure to develop programs to help him.

KRETCHMER: White businessmen object to such demands on the grounds that blacks don't deserve government considerations that aren't extended also to whites.

JACKSON: The Government aids white businesses all the time—in the areas in which they are endangered. It subsidizes airlines and railroads. It sets up tariffs to protect textile businesses from cheap foreign imports. The black man is endangered as a businessman because of his substandard education, and the Government should be offering technical and advisory services to blacks.

KRETCHMER: What kind of services?

JACKSON: There are some basic areas where the black businessman can use government help. One is feasibility studies that will tell a man if his idea is sound. Another, of course, is capital, which should be lent according to the soundness of a business idea, rather than withheld reflexively in accordance with impossibly strict notions of what constitutes "a bad risk." If a black man came up with the idea for the next generation's Xerox, he probably couldn't get the money to develop it. Next, the Government should help him get his foot in the market's door, so that the black man can at least have a fair chance. This is one area in which Operation Breadbasket has been very successful; we've got ten chain stores such as Jewel and A&P to give shelf space to black products. Then the Government should provide real vocational training. Even if a black kid, who never intends to go to college, graduates from high school, he can't fix the wiring in the house, can't run a machine, can't lay a brick. And the vocational training should apply also to those who are already running a black business. We helped increase a black man's business from $12,000 to $160,000 in four months. But he couldn't grow with it. He had to pull his business back down to the size of his mind; he had to feel the money, count it in his hands. He couldn't handle a balance sheet, couldn't write notes for working capital before his receipts came in. That man can't go to Harvard Business School—but if the Small Business Administration and President Nixon were serious, there'd be an operation Head Start for the black entrepreneur. The way it is now, a black with talent has to choose to work in the security of a big white company. And his sapped spirit will never produce anything on its own. Black businesses, on the other hand, are a step on the road to freedom. Black products are a focus for a pride in black ability. We can't just consume what the white folks decide to make for us. Consumption leads to fatness, but production leads to freedom. A producer is free to make decisions, but a man who only consumes is a prisoner whose decisions are made by others.

KRETCHMER: Breadbasket's aims, if fulfilled, seem likely to create more middle-class blacks. Do you think there will be strong class divisions between black middle and lower classes as the former get farther away from the ghetto?

JACKSON: I don't think we will have significant class divisions. No matter how wealthy he gets, the black man can rarely buy a house where he wants to; he is still subject to the whim of any white policeman who doesn't like his looks; he is still going to be tried, if accused of a crime, by a jury of his white nonpeers. And these facts bind him firmly with his destitute brother.

KRETCHMER: How do you feel about the young militants' derisive notion that every successful black is an Uncle Tom?

JACKSON: I think it's important to be sensitive to who Uncle Tom is. Uncle Tom is not our enemy. He grew up in the ghetto; he went to bad schools. He's a successful black hustler who bends and smiles before the white man in order to provide for his children. He's not a man who sits around thinking up ways to hurt black people. There's nothing wrong with a Southern boy who grew up in a shack with an outhouse wanting a real home. The jobs we once picketed to get are now being derided as Uncle Tom jobs. But the black bourgeoisie is still very close to the roots, if for no other reason than the fact that in the colonial system, he can't get too far. Blacks don't [want] good music or tasty meals. They move to white society for joy, fulfillment, get away from bad schools and apartments where the trash isn't collected. They aren't moving away from blacks but from the rats.

KRETCHMER: Are you saying that there's no disunity among blacks?

JACKSON: There is an unfortunate division among blacks now that is set off by a certain self-righteousness, a competition for being the blackest. But we must never forget that Nat Turner was middle-class, as were Frederick Douglass and Dr. King—and even Stokely Carmichael. We will not be trapped into glorifying ignorance and poverty. That will not improve the lives of black people.

KRETCHMER: Do you agree with young radicals who feel that blacks who are assimilated into the economy will become new cogs in the corporate machine?

JACKSON: We want to create a new value system that will produce a generation of black liberators, not exploiters. You can't ask a black man not to work because America's value system is perverted. But I would hope that when the black man gets a job in a company that is part of the military-industrial complex, he will organize in a union that is as concerned with basic values as it is with decent wages. Instead of producing war matériel for an unjust and immoral war, the union could pressure the company into producing goods that will help and heal people. The virtuous and vicious aspects of our economy are interrelated. We produce more food and clothing—and guns—than we need; we have the capacity to save more people from malice and disease than any other nation in the history of the world, and to kill more people than any other nation in the history of the world. No one attacks our ability to build X-ray machines or washing machines. Our national priorities are the real problem.

KRETCHMER: Can blacks change them?

JACKSON: This is the challenge of Operation Breadbasket. The businessmen we help, for example, are discouraged from getting rich and leaving the ghetto. We develop profit sharing; we try to make it our company as much as the owner's. We encourage a dialogue between owner and employee, and we encourage participatory democracy.

KRETCHMER: Can Breadbasket help blacks outside the ghetto as well as within it?

JACKSON: Yes. Let me give you an example of how it can work—a case of real soul power, where blacks had the integrity to stick out a crisis and aid one another over thousands of miles. When the most recent voting rights bill was passed, black Alabama farmers found that they weren't able to find markets for their products anymore. Whites were retaliating for their new political power. On top of that, George Wallace prevented them from borrowing money, so they couldn't expand economically, because of the combined pressures of racism and farming small plots. Instead of quitting capitalism—there were 1,500 of them—they formed the Southwest Alabama Farmers Cooperative. They planted and harvested their crops and then brought them to Chicago. We at Breadbasket then went to the supermarkets in the ghetto and told the owners that they would either put the brothers' products on the shelves or face boycotts. They accepted the produce. The brothers in Alabama could farm there and have an open outlet in Chicago. We were able to do this out of a sense of "peoplehood." That's my kind of black nationalism—blacks helping one another on a national scale.

KRETCHMER: Isn't it one of the great fears of Southern whites that blacks who outnumber them will usurp their place in society if they ever win enough economic and political power?

JACKSON: The problem here is that the poor white and the poor black have mutual fear. Poor blacks fear that if poor whites aren't eliminated, they won't be able to eat, and the poor whites feel just the same way in reverse. The historical difference is that poor whites in the South have controlled the police and the military and have thereby maintained power over the blacks. We in the Poor People's Campaign believe that the basic anxiety of whites is an irrational fear of extermination—a fear that can be removed with a guaranteed income, with guaranteed medical care and education. Dr. King was firm in his resolve that black power must be secondary to people's power. When the economic base of all the people is raised, racism will decline. As the Poor People's Campaign gets stronger, racism will lose its hold on the consciousness of the white poor.

KRETCHMER: Do you honestly think, as Dr. King did, that there's going to be a movement of the poor that will include whites, blacks, Puerto Ricans, Mexicans and Indians?

JACKSON: It's inevitable. If our good sense doesn't connect us through affirmation, then America's greed will lock us together by negation. False racial pride has divided the lower class, but we must stop defining and separating ourselves because of skin color. We should define ourselves by our economic position and shift the fight from a horizontal confrontation of poor black versus poor white to a confrontation of "have" versus "have not." Dr. King could have been the suture that connected the various bones of the bottom classes. Just two weeks before his assassination, there was a meeting of a dozen representative ethnic groups in SCLC's Atlanta office. That was the beginning of something really new, and it is continuing. For just one example, Dr. Abernathy marched with Cézar Chávez, and Operation Breadbasket supports the grape strike as if it were our own project, by boycotting and picketing Jewel Tea and other stores where California table grapes are sold.

KRETCHMER: But do you really think that the white poor are going to join you?

JACKSON: The white poor have always been distracted from demanding their rights; they've been too embarrassed to admit their deprivation. They've nourished themselves on the meager psychic diet of racism. But during the Illinois Hunger Campaign, we offered poor whites food and they digested it. In East St. Louis, Illinois, a white man named Hicks addressed a congregation of hunger marchers. Mr. Hicks has nine children and works five and six shifts of day labor a week but still can't make enough to feed his family or even to put a shack over their heads. Mr. Hicks and his family were taken in by black folks. They shared equally, and it was the first time in his life, he said, that he felt any sense of security. There are a lot more Mr. Hickses out there who just haven't realized yet that they don't have to suffer alone, that a massive cooperative effort by the poor class is the only answer. United in a class struggle, we can force the redistribution of wealth in America.

KRETCHMER: The idea of class war, hot or cold, has always been associated with the theories of socialism. Do you think of yourself as a socialist?

JACKSON: I adhere to the ideals of my religion—that the earth is the Lord's and its food was intended for all men. The trend of the world today—in Sweden, Guinea and Britain, for example—is toward some form of democratic socialism, where men eat because the ground is fertile. America stands in conflict with that trend by allowing a few people to control and distribute the food, rather than letting people eat because they are living. The truth, of course, is that this same America, where socialism is such a dirty word, is already operating in a sophisticated state of socialism for the rich, while the poor live in a crude state of classic capitalism.

KRETCHMER: Please explain that.

JACKSON: The people in this society who follow the Protestant ethic and work long hours by the sweat of their brow are the poor. They work at the hardest jobs and often still don't get enough money to pass the poverty level. Even when they try to break out, it's an attempt to start a street-corner business, where the rules of classic capitalism prevail. The poor storekeeper, for example, doesn't control his market through advertising; he can't float a bond issue and use other people's money to run his business. But the rich man has socialism. We've got 6,536 farmers in this country who receive $25,000 not to work. That's socialism. The campuses expand, chopping pieces of land out of black neighborhoods, with the financial help of the National [Defense] Education Act. Even wealthy schools for rich men's sons are state supported. The interstate highway program, none of which benefits those who can't afford a car, is 90 percent federally financed. There wouldn't be a trucking industry without government help. The list is endless and includes the oil companies and their depletion allowance, the railroads, the airlines and airports, the power companies. The rich talk about tax shelters and tariff protections, while the poor talk about sweat and blood.

KRETCHMER: But isn't welfare a form of socialism for the poor?

JACKSON: As it now stands, welfare is a form of humiliation. It is demeaning and dehumanizing. Men use money; welfare recipients use stamps. Men have privacy; welfare recipients have no privacy and can be visited any time of day or night. Their most intimate relationships can be called into question by people who are indifferent to them. Instead of abusing the poor, this nation has to understand that the welfare recipient is a product of the success of our economy. The unskilled black man whose job has been lost to technology today will be joined shortly by the unskilled white man whose job will be lost to the next technological advance. Either we see these men as having been freed by technology, perhaps to fulfill a creative role, or we see these men as having worked hard only to find themselves enslaved in poverty by the same technology. Whichever perspective one has, we must evolve a subsidy that will preserve these precious human lives, not destroy them as welfare has.

KRETCHMER: Were you encouraged by President Nixon's new welfare proposals?

JACKSON: I was thoroughly discouraged. I watched Nixon the night he delivered that welfare address. My anger was tempered only by my incredulity at the immensity of his con job. He lied for nearly an hour and didn't even crack a smile. He asked the country to think of him as a great humanitarian, but we weren't fooled. Behind all those promises is the single fact that the states are going to retain control of most of the Nixon program. When the states had the power, black people couldn't vote, couldn't ride in the front of a bus, couldn't drink from any public water fountain, couldn't use any john they wanted. Now Nixon says to Thurmond and Stennis, "Take care of them poor folks." Right this minute, there are forty states violating the welfare laws. We don't need a redistribution of welfare-disbursement stations in this country; we need a redistribution of wealth. The president challenged the poor to go to work, without saying what he would do to improve the lot of those who can't work. I'll be encouraged when the president challenges the rich to show their humanity and grant to the poor their basic rights as human beings.

KRETCHMER: The white lower middle class is becoming quite vocal about its opposition to welfare in any form for those they characterize as too lazy to work. What's your reaction?

JACKSON: The fact is that the poor work the hardest and have always done so. We made cotton king, cooked other people's food when we had none of our own, stooped to clean bathrooms. Now we are unskilled, because the schools don't teach us, because less money is spent on the education of blacks than is spent on whites. A state of despair has set in for those in the black community who have been told no too often, and perhaps they can never be healed. When white people say they know a man on welfare who is too lazy to work, I say that may be so. But the man they see is a dried-up prune. I ask them, "Did you see that man when he was a boy? Did you see him when he said, 'Momma, do you have a piece of bread?' Did you see him before hope was snuffed out by despair?" The white middle class is paying less tax money to support welfare mothers than it is to support the farm industry. I don't hear them complaining about that. The bulk of their tax money goes to subsidizing the rich and fighting wars abroad—wars fought by the sons of welfare mothers, not by the middle-class kids who go to college. The middle class invests in America with its tax dollars, but the poor have to invest their lives.

KRETCHMER: Is it possible to raise a family on the funds provided by welfare? Many claim it isn't.

JACKSON: Let me put it this way: If I give you twenty-two cents for a meal, you know pretty well what you're going to get to eat. I thought I knew what poverty was all about until I went on our hunger campaign. I saw children eating red clay. Doctors call it pica when people who don't get sufficient food eat things that have the appearance of food. I saw a mother give her child saltines and onions for breakfast and send her off to school on that. I saw a white mother with four kids, one of whom, a boy, had leukemia. He drank all the milk the family was allotted on a food stamp supplement, and it wasn't enough even for him. She took him everywhere in a little wagon, the kind kids play with. He was frail and helpless, and the mother was exhausted; the entire family looked bloodless and frightened, as if they would never have a moment's joy. I can understand why they might feel that way, living as they must with the fact that there is a ceiling on the welfare allotment but no ceiling on the rent or the food prices or the amount of tragedy a family can suffer. The insufficient welfare funds are especially damaging to babies.

Eighty percent of the brain develops during the three months immediately before birth and the first three years of life. The minds of welfare children, who cannot get enough to eat, are stricken early.

KRETCHMER: Why don't welfare allowances provide adequate support?

JACKSON: Welfare allotments tend to be about one-third of the minimal standard of living as defined by the Government. In Texas, New York, and California this year, even that meager appropriation was cut. Furthermore, rents and food prices are higher in poor areas than in middle-class areas, so the poor must spend more, even though they have less. The result of this deprivation is that the black child goes to school without breakfast, cannot afford lunch at school and cannot look forward to a decent supper at night. His hunger is such a distraction that he is not motivated to learn. All of these elements combine to place him farther and farther behind in school. He has no goals, no hero images, no sense of purpose or identity. He is physically weaker than his white contemporaries and probably sickly, because he doesn't get medical care.

KRETCHMER: Earlier, you referred to the dominance of professional sports by black athletes. That doesn't fit with the image of physical weakness you just presented.

JACKSON: Some men will thrive even in a prison camp, so it isn't surprising that you'll find an occasional black youth who overcomes his poverty. But the important reason for the dominance of black athletes is that a high proportion of black men—both those who ate well and those who didn't—directed themselves toward athletics because the field was more open to them than any other. More blacks tried to be boxers because there was no point in trying to be a bookkeeper or a mathematician. A black man whose mind might have had great aptitude for math wouldn't have been trained by a ghetto school. It made more sense for him to try to be a ballplayer, even a third-rate one, because it was so unlikely that he'd have a fair chance to be anything else.

KRETCHMER: A persistent part of the white stereotype of the black man is that he runs faster and jumps higher than whites. But some anthropologists have claimed recently that there actually are genetic differences between white and black. Will this new evidence worsen the relationship between white and black?

JACKSON: It won't affect us. The black man has never needed to believe that there are differences; that's a white man's problem. Our natures are the same. Our urges and drives as people are the same. Mankind has one father, and that's time. It has one mother, and that's nature. Both of these life processes are sound and consistent and universal. The third process is brotherhood, which is all messed up, because white folks have tried to withdraw from it. The eternal existential dilemmas of fate and death, guilt and condemnation, emptiness and meaninglessness are the same for all men. But our relationship, based upon distorted information peddled by white folks who reject the humanity of others, has been perverted.

KRETCHMER: What are the psychological and cultural differences between white and black, if any?

JACKSON: Slavery is our cultural heritage, and it should have been a thoroughly destructive one. But instead of seeing ourselves as slaves from Africa brought over to serve the lusts and wants of white people, a providential way of seeing our slavery is that we are missionaries sent from Africa by God to save the human race. Who else is in a position so close to the Pentagon, the greatest threat to the world's existence? Who else is in a position to literally redirect the most powerful economy on earth? Who else in the world is in the enemy's kitchen and his schoolroom? We are, perhaps, the only ethnic group in the world that has the power to redirect the destiny of white America. Neither China nor Russia nor France nor England could do it. I don't look for white folks to give me any direction. My experience has taught me that white people are spiritually impotent, by and large, because all they've really produced is a lot of goods and services and a lot of death.

KRETCHMER: That's a sweeping condemnation. Would you say that the late Norman Thomas, to name one of many men, was spiritually impotent?

JACKSON: No, he was certainly a spiritual man, and you could find others. The point is that such a man is not representative of the white American culture. In fact, the secondary roles that genuinely humane white people are forced to play is indicative of what I'm trying to say. Black society chooses to be led by its prophets, white society by its hustlers. The men of highest sensibility in white society find themselves rebelling from it just as blacks must rebel. America is known not for her capacity to love and heal but for her capacity to organize and kill. America has an aristocratic, military definition of man. American men judge themselves by their wealth, status and power, not by their intelligence, compassion or creativity. That's why the idea of looking for racial equality here is a farce. To become equal to white folks would be to become part of the greatest tradition of killing in the history of the world.

KRETCHMER: That might sound to some not only like a blatant overstatement, but like a proclamation of black supremacy.

JACKSON: I don't know what it sounds like, but I know what the record will indicate. There is no evidence of Africa invading Europe, of her early advanced civilizations killing or enslaving other nations. Historically, blacks have not been the aggressors in war, not even here in America. We did not mobilize to go to war for our long-overdue justice, but there have been wars of injustice waged against us. The profound men in this culture have been black—Frederick Douglass, for example, who was more pertinent than Lincoln on the subject of slavery and the liberation of mankind. And the crusader for justice in Mississippi was Medgar Evers, not Jim Eastland. In New York, Malcolm was pertinent, not Nelson Rockefeller, who did not bat an eye when he approved the welfare cuts. The one who cried out for peace in the world and meant it was not the white leader, President Johnson; it was the black leader, Dr. King. During the past fifteen years, Dr. Abernathy has been more relevant than any American president. Blacks have striven for moral dignity, and by contrast with America's state of immorality, we appear to be moral supremacists, not black supremacists.

KRETCHMER: The war in Biafra seems every bit as brutal as any other war. Black life there seems to be as cheap to blacks as you say it is to whites in this country.

JACKSON: The Nigerians and Biafrans are fighting with white men's weapons. They are fighting a war that is based on a white man's division of Africa, and the cause of the division was an earlier economic colonialism. The war is an unfortunate aberration and the signs of white meddling are everywhere in it.

KRETCHMER: During the 1968 teachers' strike in New York City, there was evidence of deep-rooted black hostility toward Jews. Is anti-Semitism consistent with your claim of black moral supremacy?

JACKSON: In the first place, there were really few examples of black anti-Semitism, and these examples were blown out of all proportion by the teachers' union, which benefited by the dissemination of fear. More significantly, though, I don't think you can characterize blacks as anti-Semites. We have never been obsessed with the Jew as Christ killer. But our relationship with the Jew has changed as the black movement has changed. When blacks began to confront the Southern white power structure, most of which was WASP Baptist and Methodist, Jews gave us great support, both financial and moral, and a real kinship developed. But once the movement moved north and the problem was defined not just in terms of social segregation but in terms of economic colonialism, the Jew began to be revealed as landlord and shop owner. Of course, he is more conspicuous than the Protestant, because his name is likely to identify his ethnic background. And he is also more sensitive: It is much easier to embarrass or humiliate a Jew than either a Protestant or a Catholic, because, unlike the others, the Jew immediately identifies with suffering.

As blacks have emerged, the Jew has been there as teacher and shopkeeper, and there has been an inevitable friction. But I think the mood of the blacks is more one of anti-colonialism than of anti-Semitism. For blacks cannot afford to be anti-people; no matter who the people are, they must be anti-evil. I think the Jews who are most concerned about anti-Semitism, however, should keep in mind that blacks have not exploited Jews at all. We have not owned anything in the Jewish community—no clothing stores, banks, food stores. The Jewish community, like most others, has a left and a right wing—some who operate in a tradition of justice and others who violate that tradition. Rather than develop a persecution complex, perhaps it ought to expend some of the energy it spends complaining about black anti-Semitism on the Jewish merchants who are known to be exploiters and tend to pull the reputation of the Jewish community down.

KRETCHMER: Jews, along with Irish, Italian and other immigrant groups, are often held up as an example that the blacks, if they were industrious enough, could emulate. The premise is that those groups were poor and lived in ghettos but were able to overcome that experience and join the American mainstream. Why hasn't that happened to blacks?

JACKSON: First, those groups came here voluntarily and were always free. We came here involuntarily and are still not wholly free. The other immigrant groups are white and could lose their identity and merge with the majority when it was necessary; with a few technical skills or a decent education, it was a simple matter for them to bypass prejudice. Their families were not destroyed and their sense of historical continuity was preserved. Most importantly, they did not suffer the tremendous color stigma of the white man.

Historically, there was a conspiracy to hold us down. We were enslaved, then locked into plantations, as we are now locked into ghettos. When America finally released our physical bonds in 1865, it was as if we had been in jail for two hundred years and were let out without a road map or a dime to go to the city. There was no attempt to help us overcome the psychological or economic hardships of slavery. Many blacks didn't survive; and of those who did, most had to pervert their natures [to] become invisible men, as Ralph Ellison wrote, become hidden, for it was too dangerous to assert one's real identity, one's manhood. No other ethnic group was faced by a hostile white society that wanted to castrate it both physically and psychologically.

KRETCHMER: Then today's black militance is a quest to resurrect that manhood.

JACKSON: One thing that I have to say right off is that there's nothing to be learned from the white man's idea of manhood. An American man is identified by his weapon, by what he controls. American men are obsessed; they are gratified by making money they can't even spend, which is a kind of emptiness of the soul. Real manhood should be defined by the ability to help and to heal, by an extension of the mind, by knowledge exerting its power over ignorance. Real manhood comes from helping others be free, by breaking the bonds of slavery.

KRETCHMER: Do you mean that metaphorically?

JACKSON: Only partly. Many of us have internalized slavery and behave like slaves, responding to the slave master when he calls. In some communities, we must fight our own people because they maintain the slave institutions. They are still in awe of Pharaoh and are afraid to confront him. That is a form of slavery. The slave psychology works on a subtle level that warps the black mind. It has been drummed into blacks that whites are the creators and producers and thinkers. Blacks whom we might have respected were taken from us.

George Washington Carver's image is one of a docile creature, an old man in a laboratory, bowing to a white child. The fact is that he developed over three hundred elements from the peanut and almost singlehandedly revived the Southern economy. A black man, Daniel Hale Williams, was the first open-heart surgeon. There are many, many other examples, but the point is that blacks never knew about them. It was easy to preserve the image of the dull-witted, slow-talking and thinking black bumbler.

There is still a need among blacks for white validation of their efforts. If Tommie Smith and John Carlos had a race tomorrow and both broke their records for the 220-meter dash, and the race were held on a black campus, where all the judges were black, black people wouldn't believe it, and neither would whites. But if it were a white track meet, there'd be no problem. As for our churches, they gave up their soul—and I mean that in both senses—to copy white church styles. That's why at Operation Breadbasket meetings, which are deeply based in religion, we have a band and a Gospel choir and consciously try to capture the rhythm of our people.

KRETCHMER: Is the slave psychology the reason for your own fieriness and emotionalism when you address a black congregation?

JACKSON: Certainly. I am seeking converts—not necessarily to religion, although there's that, too. But I want to make my people realize their own selfhood. I begin each service with a chant that says, "I am somebody." It also says, "I may be poor and I may be on welfare, but I am somebody." Because black people have to learn that they have rights just because they're alive. They've got to stop putting themselves down because of an induced inferiority complex. The slave psychology was apparent when Dr. King came out against the Vietnam War. He had all the credentials you could ask for: Nobel Prize winner, an international leader, a scholar and a Ph.D. But blacks said he had a lot of audacity; he's a preacher and should confine himself to civil rights. But when Robert Kennedy and Senator McGovern took the same position, then it was all right. And after Memphis, when SCLC's James Bevel expressed Dr. King's contempt for capital punishment, he was scorned by the black community. He said Dr. King would have wanted James Earl Ray rehabilitated, would have said to fight hatred but spare the hater. Bevel also pointed out the irony of trying to obtain justice by sacrificing a two-bit waiter for a billion-dollar black prophet. But blacks said he was crazy. Then Ted Kennedy said that Sirhan's life should be spared because his brother Robert was against capital punishment. The black community immediately cited Teddy as a great man of justice who didn't become vindictive in the face of personal tragedy. This is a painful indication of our self-contempt. We must stop looking to whites to validate our worth; we must look within for beauty and strength and courage.

KRETCHMER: Your own self-confidence, as contrasted with Dr. King's humility, seems to be of formidable dimensions, and you've been accused of messianic impulses. Do you see yourself as the next great national black leader?

JACKSON: First of all, Dr. King was not humble; he was forthright and audacious. He was killed for challenging white power. As for me, I am confident of my abilities as a social analyst, but I have no illusions of grandeur. My job is to proclaim liberty, to preach unity, to bind up broken hearts.

I am just taking care of my assignment. Besides, anyone in public life in this violent society who would make such long-range plans is a fool.

KRETCHMER: You certainly expose yourself to the risk of assassination as much as any man. Do you think that you may be subconsciously seeking martyrdom?

JACKSON: I want to live. I've got no hang-up with that. But a man must be willing to die for justice. Death is an inescapable reality, and men die daily, but good deeds live forever. An assassin believes that you can kill the dream by killing the dreamer; that is an error.

KRETCHMER: Would you have any special message to leave with black people if you were killed?

JACKSON: Yes. Don't send flowers. Don't come around with your tears. Picket. Go to PTA [Parent-Teacher Association] meetings. Fight for higher wages. If I die tonight and you wake up tomorrow, make the most of it.

KRETCHMER: You've been quite sick a few times this year, once with a form of anemia, and also with some very debilitating viruses. Yet you hardly let up on your activities, rarely sleep and constantly drive yourself toward exhaustion. Why?

JACKSON: Because I have a sense of urgency about what has to be done. It is not the thought of death so much as it is the crying need for justice. Perhaps both facts motivate me simultaneously. I do feel that I have to fulfill my work in an appointed time. I would like to sleep, but ideas come to me in the night and wake me. I think I'm drawing my stamina from a spiritual source that has been allotted to me; for that reason, I have no choice but to keep on driving. You can't devote the energy necessary to confront Pharaoh unless you are spiritually consumed by the need for liberation. But that is social consciousness, not a messianic need to be worshiped. There are some aspects of glory attached to having the privilege to lead, but none of the agony ever gets publicity, because television cameras don't record people tossing and turning in their beds at night.

KRETCHMER: Inasmuch as the Southern Christian Leadership Conference is basically a religious group, it's understandable that religion plays a large role in your life. But what appeal can the church have for a cynical twenty-year-old kid from the ghetto?

JACKSON: The black church is relevant because it has provided a home for our rebellion. It has cherished our people. The white church, on the other hand, worships worship, not Christ nor love nor brotherhood. God is very sick here; the God of justice and liberty is almost nonexistent. Christianity is universal, but the American flag flies higher than the cross in American churches; and when wartime comes, universal love goes out the window. If Americans had a true God consciousness, they could not leave the church on Sunday and shield their eyes from the hungry.

But there is extraordinary relevance in the actual

teaching of Christ. If you love people, you will not destroy them in war; if you love deeply, you will distribute the goods of the earth that the Father provided, so that people will be fed and housed. That is the Jesus I identify with. His was a program for feeding the hungry, clothing the naked and giving company to the lonely.

KRETCHMER: In the past, some critics have regarded Christianity as an impediment to black liberation; blacks were supposed to have been content to get their reward in heaven. Did you consciously evolve this activist approach to Christianity?

JACKSON: My religious philosophy can be summed up in an old Southern story about two farmers. One farmer was most concerned about his duty to God. He attended church every day and worked his fields in the afternoon. His neighbor never attended church and never paid any attention to religious rituals. The first farmer was just eking out a living; the second farmer was getting twice the harvest from a lot the same size. Finally, the first farmer said to the second, "Brother, I don't understand. I've been working this land and doing my duty for God and asking [for] His help. I go to church each day. Yet I can't get ahead at all. You never take care of your religious obligations, yet you're getting all the bounty. What am I doing wrong?" The second farmer answered, "I don't know what you're talking to God all the time for. He doesn't know anything about farming. This place didn't produce anything when He had it all to Himself." That's the whole thing. God made it but man has to go out and do it.

KRETCHMER: In our interview with Dr. King four years ago, he said the aims of SCLC were removing the barriers of segregation, disseminating the creative philosophy of nonviolence, and total integration of the Negro into American life. How much have things changed since then?

JACKSON: Four years ago, SCLC was a Southern movement primarily concerned with social segregation. Blacks were defined as less than human and were not allowed to participate in public. We were "boys" and our goal was to be recognized as men. That drive was aimed at creating a moral consciousness, and one of our slogans was "Save the soul of America." I think that one of the reasons for impatience among blacks today, and the reason for the appeal of violence, is that we never before knew just how awful the secrets locked in America's soul really were. We didn't know then that America would bomb a people to pieces and side with the oppressors in order to preserve her financial investments. We didn't know then that the Northern liberal had better manners than Bull Connor but that his institutions were no less thoroughly racist. And we didn't know then that the capitalists who slandered us with cries of "Communist" were living high off the Government hog, while we were starving in the streets.

This education of ours has led to a change of mood. Our first concern now is not white America's soul; it is Black America's body. We are justified in our impatience, because that body is hungry. When Moses had his illumination and realized that he could confront Pharaoh, the Bible says that Moses had to take his shoes off, because now he was on holy ground and the bushes were burning. Actually, the bushes were not burning; Moses was burning. His eyes were aflame—the skin had come off them. Black people today are burning: The skin is off their eyes. The movement is now in a resistance phase and we will no longer cooperate with the white slave master. Either we are going to live or America is going to die. The ghetto experience has not been a satisfying or a useful one, but it has given us inner resources—the ability to do much with very little.

I read in the white press how Black people are dispirited and confused. White editorial writers claim that the Civil Rights Movement is fragmented. That is not true; the movement is very together: The NAACP [National Association for the Advancement of Colored People], which just saved the voting rights bill, is doing its thing in Southern courts; the Urban League is doing its thing in industry; the Panthers are feeding kids in the streets; SCLC just had a political victory in Greene County, Alabama; Operation Breadbasket is thriving. It is white America that is at the crossroads. If she does not join us in the resurrection of her soul, in the fulfillment of her dream for all her people, then I foresee a day when little children in a schoolroom on the moon read in the history books about an empire that crumbled because all her power and might of arms could not cure the immoral greed that diseased her spirit.

TO BE ETHNIC, ETHICAL, AND EXCELLENT

INTERVIEW BY TONY BROWN AND DIAHANN CARROLL
BLACK JOURNAL
JANUARY 17, 1975

TONY BROWN: What are you doing these days?

JESSE JACKSON: Well, just glad to be up here in New York with y'all. We're really putting an awful lot of emphasis into dealing with the effects of this economy upon all poor people, our people in particular. I think our movement now has to have a dual focus: economic generation and spiritual regeneration.

Economic generation to the extent that we have more than six million people unemployed, twenty-five million people making less than $3,000 a year, another twenty-five million less than six thousand, another twenty-five million, less than nine thousand. Given the inflated economy, that means that you have three levels of real poverty in the country, so that is a critical question.

On the other hand, we have a kind of deteriorating spiritual condition in the black community where our young people are trapped, pushing dope in their veins rather than hope in their brains, and pickling their brains with liquor, and using all kinds of ways to escape reality. It is at that level that we must be spiritually regenerated, because if we have a new school and don't have the will to learn, it's to no avail. If we got a job and don't have the will to work, or we have the opportunity and can't seize it because we've tripped out. It is at that level we must have a dual focus. I guess biblically speaking, you would say that man cannot live by bread alone. You need the bread and the spiritual development.

The question becomes, How do you break such a recession as this? Number one, you point to the weaknesses of it. The inflation that we're now on is not a consumer-inspired inflation where people have spent too much, but rather because the superrich and the military budget have been made into sacred cows. Ford says he's going to save $5 billion in surtax. Well, the fact is the military budget's growth is $7 billion a year. Why is that $7 billion sacred? You ask people making $15,000 a year to tighten up their belts—well, they're already wearing suspenders because their real income has been eaten up by inflation. Then he says that if we save $20 billion from federal spending, we can break stagflation. Well, the Proxmire report indicates that the military spent, beyond its appropriations last year, $27 billion. Now that plus the superrich not being taxed properly and being allowed to develop monopolies and run competition out of business, that is why the economy is jammed.

On the one hand, we must know that. On the other hand, we must prepare to hit these streets marching again in mass. January 15th this year, which is Dr. King's birth date, we're going to celebrate it by marching in at least fifty cities simultaneously. Marching, I might add, behind the Hawkins full employment bill, demanding that once and for all that it's declared in this country, that everybody has a right to a job, a decent house, and medical care. In my judgment, that's where the struggle is now. It's not as much civil rights as it is silver rights. It's a matter of redefining the economy.

BROWN: You know, I heard him, Diahann, in Chicago at his annual Black Expo, and you've made a very interesting parallel, as you do often, your "three Es."

JACKSON: Well, my point is that we must be *ethnic*, which is our blackness, and accept our African roots, our African heritage. Get all of the psychological self-esteem that we need out of being black. Have our natural hairdos and our symbols of blackness.

But you've got to go beyond being ethnic; you must also be *ethical*. Cain and Abel were ethnic—they were two brothers, came out of the same mother's womb—but they were not ethical, and so they killed each other. In addition to being ethnic, you must be ethical.

Beyond that, you must be *excellent*, because in the last analysis, the only thing that will protect you from genocide is to be necessary. I mean, whether you're in America or in Africa and wherever, your life chances are increased by being excellent. Now, you may not survive even if you are excellent, but you're almost guaranteed to get wiped out if you're not excellent. I mean that which has protected Hank Aaron, and that which protected Willie Mays, that which has sustained Muhammad Ali, that which has made a rare bunch go down into the annals of science, George Washington Carver, is in spite of a racist society not liking their ethnicity, their excellence was of such until even their enemies had to respect where they were coming from.

BROWN: What do you think of [Nelson] Rockefeller as vice president?

JACKSON: Well, I think it's a bad choice for the country. Basically, I think it's bad because at one level there is a very delicate balance of power in this country between labor, business, and government. When a man with that much concentrated economic wealth is one heartbeat away from the presidency, it destroys that balance of power.

Beyond the way he handled an Attica situation, which becomes murder, in my judgment. It's bad that that thing happened. But even if, one, we're not coming out of our black emotional concern and ethical concern for Attica, it is not good for this government, because there are some places where this government politically should not be where he personally already is. So, there's a collision course between the interests of the country and the interests of the Rockefeller family. I think that it's a bad situation.

I would hasten to add, however, that if Rockefeller and Ford have their team, and if Nixon is resurrected, it is not racism will stop us as much as cynicism will. We can overcome Rockefeller, and Bilbo, and Maddox, and all of that bunch if we just don't give up. That is what kind of frightens me about this kind of cynical reasoning about "Blacks can't make it." I contend that the system is not good, but we can make it if anybody can, because we can do what other folk can do.

Now, if we have integrity, not only will we make it, we will change it also. But I cannot accept a set of reasons why we can't finish school, a set of reasons why our track men can't win the race, of why our boxers can't win the boxing match. We can accept no reason. We have fought racism because we never allowed cynicism to overtake us. I think when one looks at the struggles you've had with this show, I mean, racism has tried to jam you, but if you had moved and become cynical, then even if racism had moved, you still couldn't have conducted your show.

BROWN: I had a little slogan once. I asked some of my students, "If racism quit, could you take advantage of it?"

JACKSON: Oh, that's the fundamental proposition. I mean that's the case of Muhammad Ali. Racism took his title, but they didn't take his manhood. And so, when racism stepped out of the way, he didn't step back in the ring three hundred pounds and slow, because he kept his head together. At that level, you know, since preachers always develop their sayings—

BROWN: Speaking of preachers, let me ask you a preacher question: Flip Wilson brings a whole phenomenon into focus and that is the responsibility of the black artist to black people et cetera and so forth. Now we know black artists have to eat, et cetera, and so forth, and it's the old runaround about, "How much of this can I do, and how much of this?" He's been doing the Reverend Leroy, and—

JACKSON: The question is, Who are you going to eat? Are

you going to eat animals, or are we going to eat each other? I think that when we make the kind of move that he has made relative to the black church that he has moved into the area of the sacred. Jewish comedians crack a lot of funny jokes, but it's never about the rabbi. The Catholic comedians cracked a lot of jokes, but it is never about the pope. In other words, there is something sacred. I think there's a lot of room to tell jokes and finger pop and make people laugh. I'm not one of the great critics of Amos and Andy, because it was funny to me, and it didn't give me no brain damage, either.

But I think there are some areas that are basically sacred, and I think that our group of menaces, we're going to meet with that brother and try to arrive at some understanding, because on the one hand, we don't want to undercut him because—

DIAHANN CARROLL: This meeting is not taking place in a dark alley, I hope.

BROWN: We know how you Baptist preachers meet with people.

JACKSON: I tell you what, because on the one hand, I respect Flip, because he has done a lot for our cause. He's done a lot of benefits, and he's tried hard. He put a lot of black folk on that show who otherwise never would have been on television.

BROWN: But he says that his portrayal of Reverend Leroy does not in any way damage the image of black preachers.

JACKSON: Well, you see, we disagree, and that's why we have to have a meeting, but not a meeting based in hostility. When we have differences, we must reconcile our differences through dialogue and like civilized people. In the final analysis, it will not hurt us because that which he's portraying is not the truth. It won't hurt preachers, but it may hurt our children who don't know any better. Somebody needs to know the first piece of property bought in America by blacks was bought by the black church. That the first black bank, first black insurance company, first black college, Wilberforce University, black church. We talk about Harriet Tubman and the Underground Railroad: The black church was the railway station. We talk about Denmark Vesey being hung in South Carolina: The AME [African Methodist Episcopal] Church also was put out of South Carolina because that was his headquarters. We talk the civil rights legislation that was led by Adam Powell and Dr. King. These were black preachers. And so, if our black children get trapped thinking that the black preacher is Reverend Leroy, and think the black pimp is some kind of hero, it reverses their psyche. What he's doing, it may appear to be funny, but it's more dangerous than it is funny.

So, we need to discuss this. I'm not even sure he understands this history. All the ramifications of his actions. I would not suggest that we need to get nasty and hostile and try to jam him relative to NBC, but to appeal to him the reason. Just like I may do something that's out of line, and I'm on TV and rapping and talking and stuff, I would hope that you would have the capacity to come to me as a rational, concerned brother or sister without having to become anti-me.

CARROLL: But there is another point that I think is absolutely valid, and I'm not sure how I feel about this. I only know that it's important for us to be able to find the areas of ourselves where we can laugh. I think humor has saved us many, many times. The fact that you are discussing all of the pluses and all of marvelous men that you just discussed—that I was not aware of until you just made me aware of them—as menaces is another point.

You see, Flip, to me, has made another point, and you're not gonna tell me I have never seen Reverend Leroy, because I have. I was raised partially with a Reverend Leroy. Reverend, the only thing I'm saying is that there are two sides to that coin, and I believe Flip is representing one side of it. Now, is it his responsibility to represent both sides of it? Is that what you're saying?

JACKSON: I happen to think that that is a rather sacred area, that it's off limits. We know that the typical relationship between black worshiper and black church is not one of unserious stupidity. It is like taking the pimple on the face and magnifying it and calling the pimple the face and calling the face the pimple.

We have no reason to disregard, however raggedy it is, if it kept our folks' souls together, if it kept our women from jumping out of doors, if it became the place where, literally, our spiritual witch doctors kept our minds together, then it's hallowed ground for us. I contend that it's not your aptitude, but your attitude that determines your altitude, how high you're gonna get. We must have a certain attitude about something sacred. Without having something sacred, then if we disrespect the black church, we disrespect a school, we disrespect each other, we disrespect ourselves, where does respect emanate from? Where's the getting-off point for respect?

CARROLL: I see exactly what you're saying. It's just that I am not positive that we're talking about a man who disrespects religion. I think he has found an area that was humorous and you are taking exception with his presenting that area.

JACKSON: I'm also trying to be awfully kind about it. I like him personally. I relate to Flip very well, and the reason why I said I will always support him is because he has been so generous to this cause. At that level, I'm not cutting into his person.

CARROLL: Then again, you are building up my point, and that is that the man is able to see both sides of the thing. I mean, if he can do that for your cause, he most certainly sees the good of it, and knows the good of it, and is willing to make his life part of that. But he also sees the other side of it, which does have some humor in it.

JACKSON: But the effect of that which he is doing goes beyond where his contributions come in. My only contention is that there is a disagreement over that area and that we're going to have a brother to talk and try to arrive at an area. I would not like to see, every time he comes on television, black preachers and black churches feeling the urge to try to boycott or picket his show. I don't think that we need to get into that. I think that civilized people short of warfare can develop some living peace or *detente.*

CARROLL: Well, we also need more shows on the air so that we don't have just Mr. Wilson to, you know—if there were more blacks on television.

BROWN: We're at the end of the program, and there's never enough time for the country preacher. And I'd like to thank you very much, Reverend Jesse Jackson, for coming and being our guest. Thank you very much.

JACKSON: Thank you for letting me come on.

JACKSON'S PLAN STRESSES NEGOTIATIONS, NOT ARMS

INTERVIEW BY RONALD SMOTHERS
THE NEW YORK TIMES
DECEMBER 28, 1983

RONALD SMOTHERS: What do you think is the most important problem facing the United States over the next decade? And what new ideas do you have for dealing with it?

JESSE JACKSON: There's within this country a growing sense of insecurity within, the American people feeling unprotected. Many people are feeling unprotected by law, that the Justice Department is not committed to justice. There's been a cutback in this Administration on the enforcement of laws vital to the civil rights of American citizens. Women did not get an equal rights amendment passed. For blacks and Hispanics the Voting Rights Act has not been vigorously enforced. Workers are victims of plants closing without notice. Slave labor markets abroad undercut the American worker and there is the feeling that the American worker can't do anything about it, that when you're violated, you can't go to the Justice Department. So one of the first commitments that an American president must make is to adequately fund the Justice Department and fully enforce the law. For the injustice comes from unenforced laws.

For example, if the Voting Rights Act was enforced in the South adequately and you could end the second primary in the 10 Deep South states, where 53 percent of all blacks live, and there is only one black college person out of 115 and no statewide officials 18 years later. Of course at that rate, it would take 190 years to achieve parity. But if the Voting Rights Act is enforced, that is section 2, which bans forms of discrimination; if section 5 is enforced and registrars are accessible, and you end second primaries which keep black people, Hispanics, women and poor people from a securer justice, you'll get twelve to twenty black, Hispanic and female congresspersons by next November. If that happens, we'll get our share of legislators and judges and other officials, that will trigger the passage of [the] ERA [Equal Rights Amendment]. Women will all be protected in the South if the Voting Rights Act is enforced, and they are our natural allies. Since 70 percent of all poor children live in a house headed by a woman where there is no man, to enfranchise women is to protect the children. The women who go out into the workforce will then end right-to-work laws because you have the power to do so. Thus workers will get paid for their work. Most people who are poor are not on welfare. They're either too proud to apply for welfare or they otherwise work and don't get paid enough for their work.

SMOTHERS: So, the key to ending this feeling of being unprotected, the first step is to enforce the Voting Rights Act, and things will flow from that?

JACKSON: Which empowers the poor. When you empower the poor, they then have self-determination and they deal from the ability to protect themselves, so the poor in that instance do not need to be embellished. They need to be empowered. They don't need so much aid. You know, people need aid when trade is cut off. People need aid when they are otherwise disallowed the ability to protect themselves, so that's what's most important now. Second to that is the need for peace. Peace must have justice as its content and its center.

UNITED STATES-SOVIET RELATIONS

SMOTHERS: How would you go about obtaining peace?

JACKSON: Just as the first item of business for Eisenhower was to go to Korea and to risk the danger of being misunderstood, even risk failure, the risk for peace was worth it. The risk of bringing the boys back home was worth it. The boldness with which Kennedy went to Geneva to meet Khrushchev, or Nixon by going to China, or Carter by convening Camp David—we need an American president who will be glad to meet the head of the Soviet Union anywhere, any time, unconditionally but only agree conditionally. We must give the world an impression that we have a peace policy, though we have a military capability, and that we will not allow the hotline on the desk of the White House to go unused. But we must take bold steps for peace the day before so there will not be a day after. When leaders talk together the tension is relieved. When they talk, they act. And when they act they change things. Only an agreement between the president of this country and the head of the Soviet Union will give them the security to then convince their constituencies to begin to roll back the arms buildup, so peace really begins in the mind of two leaders in this instance.

THE FEDERAL DEFICIT

SMOTHERS: How serious is the growing federal deficit and specifically what would you do to reduce it? Would you raise taxes? Cut domestic spending? Cut defense spending?

JACKSON: The federal deficit is very serious. It is undermining economic growth. Under this Administration, the federal deficit is the largest it has been in the history of the country, in part because we're not generating enough tax revenue to keep us out of the deficit. And the deficit is creating the need to borrow money that is mortgaging the future of our children and having an impact of drying up money in the private economy and therefore driving up interest rates. You must first deal with what has caused the budget deficit.

One, Reaganomics. The $750 billion tax cut over a three-year period was so severe that it traumatized the economy and triggered us into the longest recession we have gone through since the Great Depression. It was so severe after two years, until the third year they cut it by $100 billion. It was projected to be $750 and it's now $650 billion. Combine Reaganomics with the Federal Reserve Board's tight money policy, which of course drove up interest rates.

Number two, the $1.8 trillion military budget, the largest that the world has ever known. This is a five-year budget, with a projected cost overrun of $600 to $750 billion. This data comes from the Congressional Budget Office. The massive recession has us now at 8 to 9 percent unemployment, higher than when Mr. Reagan came in office. For every 1 percent unemployment, it costs $30 billion. Reagan used unemployment with which to fight inflation. The combination of Reaganomics where the corporations get the big tax break without any obligation to reinvest in the economy or to reindustrialize the economy or to retrain the workforce. So, in a sense you had a dual, a double hemorrhage. Money going out of one part of the national body, corporate incentive, and money going out the other part of the body, the national body, for the massive military budget. The answer in part is the real commitment for full employment. Put America back to work. The need to build, end the slums and build houses and hospitals and build trains and a massive transit system, that would be worth a high-production economy.

SMOTHERS: The increase in job-producing investment, what would that do in terms of the deficit? Can you quantify that?

JACKSON: First of all, you should correlate the tax incentive with reinvestment in this economy. It's when you're not hemorrhaging the economy. You correlate tax incentive, the price a corporation must pay for the tax investment is to reinvest in this economy. And retrain the workers and reindustrialize also, with the commitment to have the freedom to invest because our economy needs to expand. We have to make the American worker secure. We have to make the American economy secure. In the 1960s we had a 4.8 percent unemployment and inflation was only 2.8 percent at the time. It was similar in the Eisenhower years. Because we had a Federal Reserve Board with a low interest rate. They are a factor in that, and you've simply got to invest some money to make money. That's why there's the high production cut. You got to invest in people. And invest in rebuilding American cities. Invest in hospitals, invest in having a competitive private economy. In the last twenty years we have lost our competitive edge in auto, steel, electronics, rubber and textiles. So where is the money? The money is in low interest rates, and you invest in rebuilding America. And the money is in the tax breaks that we're not getting returns on. The money is in the waste dimension of the military budget, and we have whole weapons systems that are obsolete.

THE MILITARY BUDGET

SMOTHERS: Could you name some in particular that you feel are obsolescent?

JACKSON: You got your MX missiles and B-1 missile, and I think we should freeze the military budget at this point. We oughta have a freeze so that you would have a zero real growth in the next five years and that would save $250 billion. A commitment to a peace policy and not just a war policy would save money. The more vigorously that we negotiate and resolve tension diplomatically, the less need we have to keep escalating the building of war materials. A nuclear freeze would save money.

We need to reduce the size of the ground forces in Europe. Also, our NATO [North Atlantic Treaty Organization] alliance must now pay their share. And Japan must pay its share.

SMOTHERS: To eliminate the loopholes as you said and the cuts in defense spending, a freezing of the defense budget, does that mean that you do not see any need for any increased taxation and that you don't see a need for cuts in domestic spending?

JACKSON: Well, no, there's no need at this point for cuts in domestic spending. Right now, we need to invest more in education. And invest more in job training. Because our capacity to compete in the future has a lot to do with our children's ability to compete with Honda and Toyota, Sony and Panasonic and Mitsubishi and Mercedes-Benz and the Germans and others making transit systems. So the education investment is a sound investment. Because of course, look at the causes of the inflation. The oil jolts, which we can develop reserves to reduce the impact of those jolts. The price of foods which in part had to do with a deal we cut with the Russians and lost our grain reserves. The Vietnam War. We stopped building houses. Skyrocketing medical costs. These were the factors that created inflation in the first place. And so there has to be a policy that takes into account these problem areas. Now we are still in the development of our program which has specific budgets. We know the areas for the adjustments that need to be made.

NEED FOR "A PEACE POLICY"

SMOTHERS: How much growth, after inflation, should there be in the military budget? And which weapons programs, proposed by President Reagan, would you alter? You did indicate that you favor a freeze in the military budget.

JACKSON: A nuclear freeze and regather the MX missile and the B-1 bomber and nerve gas. And you could freeze the budget and get a more efficient use of the budget allocation that's already there. You reduce the waste, and reduce the cost overrun and you still substantially have a basic body of money that we just don't have now.

We can save billions of dollars from the military budget and increase our security. Our problem is the president has a war policy and a weapons policy when what we need is a peace policy.

Some examples of savings. If we freeze the military budget in real terms over five years we will save over $250 billion from Reagan's budget proposals for fiscal year '84 and '88. Congressional Budget Office is the source of our data.

But these are not enough. We need a peace policy which allows us to reduce the dangerous nuclear arsenals and decrease exposure of our men abroad. One, the Soviet Union has stated it might accept a nuclear freeze. A freeze would increase our security. It would save over $50 billion over the next five years. Two, we've spent one-third of our military budget on defending Europe against the threat of Soviet invasion that even the NATO commander in chief says is unlikely. He says the true threat is political intimidation and division among the allies. But it is our weapons policy that causes division.

We need a peace policy, then, which would allow us to unite our allies and decrease our spending. An effective peace policy will allow us to reduce our force in Europe and save billions of dollars.

We've been sold a bill of goods about national security.

Since 1945 we've spent over $3 trillion, more than any other country, on the military. And we are less secure now than we were then. Mere military spending cannot make us secure. Only a peace policy can. The president wants us to spend over $300 billion on military threats abroad; over 45 percent of the American people are afraid to walk one mile from their house after dark.

SMOTHERS: What steps would you take to reduce tensions with the Soviet Union?

JACKSON: We must relate to Russia on terms other than just military character. We have agricultural superiority. Technological superiority. Cultural exchange. Media exchange. The American people know too little about the Soviet Union. And the more we know each other, the more we can have a mutual appreciation of each other's ways and means to survive. With the Soviet Union our course must be that of coexistence and not co-annihilation and it must be a policy that takes into account that we can, we need not, our objective is not to proselytize them or to convert them, really, not to proselytize them. But to coexist with them and to expand our trade relations.

MIDDLE EAST POLICY

SMOTHERS: What would you do differently than President Reagan to seek an overall Middle East settlement?

JACKSON: The president of the United States ought to have access to all the leaders of nations in the Middle East and ought to talk with, if he chooses to and when he chooses to, all warring factions.

America has a vital interest in peace in the Middle East. We have a moral interest because people are there. Economic interest, we get so much of our energy from them. Military interest, because of the geopolitical position. An interest because of the Persian Gulf, because their borders will take us to the Soviet Union. America has an interest in protecting Israel's right to exist in security within internationally recognized boundaries. America also has an interest in Palestinian justice, or self-determination, or a homeland for Palestinian people. The more nomadic and desperate the Palestinians are, the more tension is put upon Israel. But Israeli weapons are inadequate to defend against desperate people who will either use kamikaze or terroristic methods as a way of fighting back. We have an interest in the nonpartitioning of and the territorial integrity of Lebanon. The normalized ties with all Arab nations.

SMOTHERS: How is President Reagan not pursuing policies which adhere to those three interests?

JACKSON: When the president, in a negotiation with Mr. Shamir, did not link that negotiation with a commitment on Golan Heights, West Bank occupation, expanded settlements, and the offensive use of American weapons in the invasion and occupation of Lebanon, by the president of this country not correlating a link in the negotiations with those violations, it made America a party to the occupation and to the invasion. In effect America helped to finance that invasion and occupation which robbed America of any innocence or any moral authority. It took away from America the role of a neutral peacekeeping force and therefore made our boys the object of the hostility, more so than against the other nations that were there. And that's why our marines were the object of the raid. I think that we should support either nonaligned nations or UN peacekeeping forces to be there. America cannot serve the role of an effective peacekeeping force in Lebanon. So much so that President Reagan has now shifted the role of American marines there from peacekeeping forces to combat forces without authorization from Congress and therefore stands in violation of the War Powers Act. Because he did not get permission from the Congress, he's asking the marines to fight a war with inadequate equipment or materiel or manpower. Thus, the Syrians have us terribly outmanned in that arrangement. We're trying to offset the lack of manpower by increasing technical warfare, which has bombs dropping terribly close to Syria, which has us about seventy-five miles away from a major war with Syria, which could trigger the Soviet Union in a most direct way.

We have an obligation to support Israel's right to exist for security, not to support her right to occupy and expand. And America ought to be the first to take the initiative to get out of Lebanon and to prevail upon Israel to go back with a guarantee of keeping Israel's borders and boundaries secure and then use our diplomatic leverage to get Syria to go back to Syria.

Given the Gemayel Government, this Government and Israel and Syria and Lebanon should go to Geneva and come out of the Druse mountains of Lebanon. Presently, Mr. Reagan is escalating tensions there with his threats and increased matériel. When last month Mr. Shamir went back to Israel with an armful of weaponry and a commitment to more weaponry and Mr. Gemayel went back empty-handed, it further tilted American Middle East policy and it was provocative and therefore the fighting with Syria was predictable. The bottom line is more Americans were killed and now Lieutenant Goodman is a prisoner of war, an undeclared war in Syria.

The paradox is that the best way to defend Israel is to relieve Israel of having so many enemies. And you bring about some of this relief by bringing about a measure of fairness and justice in those relationships.

If America used its strength to get the PLO [Palestine Liberation Organization] and others to recognize Israel to exist and Israeli leaders to move toward a mutual recognition policy which I'm convinced forces like the Peace Now and the Labor Party would go for. If Israel were relieved of the tension that comes as the result of being the object of the anger of so many people, Israel could become the capital of commerce in the Middle East. Israel would be exporting talent and businesses and training. The flower in the desert could bloom all over the desert. Because Israel really is the most brilliant flower in God's garden.

SMOTHERS: Would that flowering of Israel as a force in the Middle East simply come about by these kinds of approaches? Wouldn't we have to rewrite a lot of fairly recent history for that to be possible?

JACKSON: No, I have a lot of confidence in the power of the American president operating with a moral mandate. One would have thought it was impossible to get Egypt and Israel around a bargaining table at Camp David, and surrogates couldn't bring that meeting about—only an American president.

That's why the no-talk policy toward the PLO has been a bad policy, because it has deprived the American president of the ability to reduce Israel's enemies. If Carter could not have talked to Sadat because Egyptians had killed some Israelis, he couldn't have had Camp David, and so—the Israelis maintain the right to talk to the PLO. They may choose not to. Apparently they did talk with Arafat to get the prisoners of war released and to get the Palestinians freed. So when they talked, when the Israelis and the PLO talked, in fact, lives were saved. Some Israelis were released from prison—some Palestinians were released from prison. When they talked lives were saved. In the absence of talk lives are almost always lost, and I'm really convinced that an American president could be the negotiating force via the economic, military and social security that both parties need to have a mutual recognition policy. And that is at the heart, the Palestinian question remains at the heart of the Middle East agony.

CENTRAL AMERICAN POLICY

SMOTHERS: What do you think of President Reagan's policy in Central America, and what would you do differently?

JACKSON: First of all, we should see Central America as our next-door and not our back door, which would end the contemptuous attitude toward them. Second, we must have a good neighbor policy—a next-door neighbor policy—and see Central America as essentially our allies.

SMOTHERS: What do you mean, contemptuous attitude?

JACKSON: Well, essentially as when Reagan says that they're in our back door. It's our next door. That language—psycholinguistically it expresses a certain measure of contempt—no different than [Edwin] Meese not seeing hungry people or some of the things that finally got Watt run out.

We believed that we could finance the rebels to overthrow the Government of Nicaragua, the Sandinistas. We are now losing—we're losing that war, and losing prestige and respect because of our identification with the rebels. We as a nation know too well that we helped the reign of terror and tyranny of the Somoza regime upon those people. Rebellion by the peasants was inevitable. Although the Sandinista Government is less than perfect—I met with their minister of culture just two weeks ago; they're moving toward having free elections early next year, in February or in March. America could use its strength there to accept that government even where it's possible to overcome the friction of the rebels and the Sandinista—even be a part of helping to referee or negotiate a relationship that would maximize the security of all forces involved. But the people have a right to self-determination. They have a right to their own government, and governments in transition often have military phases. I mean this country first started—not with a democracy—it was with General George Washington. Our own Government started under military rule and grew into a democracy. Democracy is the most mature form of government. It takes time to get there. When this Government embraces the landed gentry of El Salvador, we're misreading history. And to separate aid—I mean to not link aid with a human rights policy—sends a signal around the world of our noncommitment to fairness.

We should again use our strength to negotiate and use our aid as a leverage in bringing about more peaceful relations in El Salvador. The approach of gunboat diplomacy, big-stick diplomacy, nuclear threat, military exercises off of the coast, is a bad approach. And it is the assumption in time that we can officially oppress an idea whose time has come, but it will not happen. If there's any message that Christmas has it is that you may lock hope out of the inn, it can even flourish in the stable. An idea whose time has come can live under the most adverse of conditions, and the people who have been victims of a banana republic—their time for independence and self-determination and self-government has come.

GALVANIZING THE DISAFFECTED

INTERVIEW BY HENRY HAMPTON

EYES ON THE PRIZE II: AMERICA AT THE RACIAL CROSSROADS 1965–1985

APRIL 11, 1989

HENRY HAMPTON: Let me take you back to 1980. It's May of 1980. The verdicts have come in on the policeman who killed Mr. McDuffie, and one of America's worst riots takes place. You go back there. Why did you go to Miami, and what did you hope to accomplish?

JESSE JACKSON: Because there was a need, and people with whom I had worked across the years were crying out for help for fear there would be even more killing and more rioting. There are two dimensions of the Miami scene as I reflect upon it. One is its history of being one of the places where African people landed. From West Africa to South America, Brazil to the Caribbean, to the forts in Florida and Virginia, up, up the coast. It's a long and proud history of African Americans in Miami. Also, because it is so close to Latin America and to the Caribbean, there's a great sense of internationalism in Miami, a port city. In the deepest days of segregation there was some sense of a thriving African American community in southern Florida. Then with the Cold War with Cuba, African Americans were made third-class citizens. Whites were first-class citizens in terms of access and opportunity. Cubans, in some sense, were encouraged to come here in the struggle with Castro, to undercut Castro, and thus there was this kind of subjugation. Many promises made, almost no promises kept.

Why no economic development? Well, you see, a highway cut through the community, which undercut them economically and humiliated them, because they did not have the political power to fight back and to protect themselves. Banks and savings and loans companies were redlining the communities. No money was available for affordable housing, medium or small businesses. There was a great sense of economic exploitation, but strangely enough, even in the riots of the sixties, never did pure poverty incite a riot. It was always some police, people, spark, that set the flame into explosion, and that's exactly what happened when [Arthur] McDuffie was killed in 1980.

HAMPTON: When you were there in Overtown, you stayed with a Black family in Liberty City. Can you recall any impression or story that gives us some insight into how people felt?

JACKSON: Well, you know, the people are basically conservative, Christian, patriotic, but also humiliated. These were not people looking for trouble. They were looking for a job, looking for respect, looking for protection, and they found none of that, and while the Government made provisions to bring the Cubans in, they never made any provisions to allow the African Americans who lived there to maintain a standard of living or to grow. You had a very high unemployment rate among the youth, inadequate job training, almost no program for building affordable housing, so what you saw in the riot really were voices of despair, the voices of the unheard. People with their backs against the wall, particularly the young, lashed out and fought back. In part I went there because of my concern and fear that they would simply be slaughtered, that they would be killed without any sense of mercy.

Also, at that time Mr. Carter was the president, and there was a bit more sensitivity. I recall President Carter sending a team of people—Ernie Green and Lamond Godwin, Alexis Herman—a team of people from the White House to analyze what could happen in the short term in terms of some immediate relief. So, there was a certain sensitivity from the White House, but there had been no *program* there that would provide any kind of economic parity.

When Europe was down and had to be developed, they offered twenty-year, 2 percent, long-term loans, government secured. That was the heart of the Marshall Plan: not just grants, the chance for economic growth and development. Well, the Miamis of our nation never got that kind of consideration, never got that development, and even to this day, it remains a tinderbox.

HAMPTON: Given that you stayed with the people in Miami, were you buoyed by their sense of hope?

JACKSON: I was, but also, I wanted to share with them my sense of presence and concern. I also knew that because I had been there many times before, that my presence there would attract the media in some measure. The media became their form of protection, because the elements that would gun them down in a violent way had to deal with them differently with the lights on.

We also met with the editorial boards trying to interpret the crisis, because sometimes in the excitement, the media can incite more of a crisis in a given community. What these people basically wanted was their civil rights, the right to an education, the right to a job, the right to a decent house, the ability to walk their streets in safety and security.

HAMPTON: Tell me more about Miami.

JACKSON: When I think about the cities of great joy in the heart of the segregated South—Charlotte, North Carolina; Atlanta, Georgia; Augusta, Georgia, where James Brown and Leon Austin and the Buicks, that's where the quintet came from; New Orleans—but Miami was a great source of joy and excitement in part because of the weather, in part because it was an international city, but also there was a thriving African American business community in Miami that was decimated with urban removal.

I also recall that in Miami there was a Holiday Inn near the airport. It was the first Holiday Inn in America where African Americans could stay, and all of the golfers, the professional golfers, Charlie Sifford and Joe Louis and all of them, would go once a year to the great tournament in Miami in February. There was something special about being able to go to Miami and stay in the Holiday Inn and go to the tournament and go to the racetrack, or take trips from Miami and go to the Caribbean or go to South America. There was a certain sense of joy and hope there, and Miami was torn asunder with no sense of replacement, no sense of hope and development. These riots are almost always expressions of despair and desperation.

HAMPTON: Once the Black community began in Chicago to react to Byrne excesses, how, how did PUSH begin to work with organizations and what was your role?

JACKSON: You know, you really must put the Chicago scene within the context of a glorious history. I mean Oscar De Priest, one of our first African American congresspeople from Chicago, Bill Dawson from Chicago, the Daley-Dawson combination which delivered for Kennedy the presidency in 1960, and then the modern period would have to be Dr. King coming to Chicago, leading open-housing marches, and that's when I really emerged on the scene. I had been with him as had many others in Selma in '65, the year before, and he made the judgment really based on appeal by Al Raby and Bill Barry and a combination of people to come to Chicago. It was said that you could not expose segregation in the North because it was subtle. The fact is, it was everything except subtle. It was dynamic. It was real, blatant, ugly, violent. And as he marched toward Gage Park and, and marched toward the southwest, bricks were thrown, and there was this great confrontation between the police and the residents there, because they had somehow been taught that African Americans were dirty, and indecent, and violent. They had these fears. Their fears had not been relieved, and there was a struggle for an empowered political community, the Silent Six.

Dr. King began to give voice to those fears and frustrations in Chicago. Then Mayor Daley died, and one of his loyal servants, Wilson Frost, was the mayor pro tem, should have been acting mayor. They locked him off of the fifth floor of city hall. Well, then [Michael A.] Bilandic was given that job in that arrangement. Mayor Byrne beat him but in part because a significant number of independents, African Americans, Hispanics, progressive whites went with Jane Byrne and she had a little pizzazz, a little gusto, and we knew it was a break. I remember when several aldermen who went with her for the first time said, "Now that she has won, she has met with George Dunne and that group before meeting with us. We are afraid."

There was a meeting in my office with Harold Washington and several aldermen. They said, "We need somebody to help us," and so Harold and, I think, Nancy Jefferson, two or three of us, went down to Jane Byrne's transition office, and after meeting with her it was so clear that she had no special sense of obligation to the element that made the break to elect her.

Harold said, "We're going to have trouble with her administration unless something fundamental changes." There was a sense that we had to keep organizing because we had not yet been recognized with parity, that we were still somehow less than peers, and so the organization continued. Because she had a lot of exciting activity—ChicagoFest—and because she did reach out in ways that, say, Daley and Bilandic never had, there was a sense that somehow you couldn't beat her. She was female. She was not hostile. She was not polarizing the city, per se, and yet we were not involved in the equation.

Right after Jane Byrne was elected, the aldermen who had gone the independent route and supported her, who had won, felt that they should have access to see her immediately. Her first meeting was with George Dunne and the forces that we had defeated. They felt very insecure and had a meeting in my office. In that meeting was Harold Washington, in that meeting was Nancy Jefferson, and the combination of us, we said, "Let's get an appointment with her."

Well, since I had endorsed her publicly the Saturday before and she had gone downtown saying I was a significant leader, whatever that meant, I called her and was able to get through. When we met with her, there was a sense that there was not the traditional hostility, but not the sense of partnership, the sense of parity, the sense of mutuality. Harold Washington said, "We're going to have trouble with this administration. We must really keep, keep pressing forward."

Because she ran an administration that was not polarizing and was not hostile and ugly, it was very difficult to get a grip on it. But one day, Dorothy Tillman, Marion Stamps, and Lu Palmer went to a Chicago Housing Authority meeting, where you have this tremendous number of African American, Hispanics, and poor people living, but no real power on the Chicago Housing Authority Board, and they were arrested. I went to help get them out of jail, as well as some other people. I had become exhausted with what to do to really get people's attention, to galvanize them.

I did this weekly radio show, and on this Sunday morning,

someone called and said, "Well, Jesse, why don't you guys just boycott her coronation? The ChicagoFest really was just her coronation, her pretense for running for reelection."

I wanted to say, "Brother, you don't understand. Organizing a boycott against the ChicagoFest with all of the money involved and the big artists coming and the high expectation, people coming from all around the country to ChicagoFest . . ." I couldn't say he was wrong, but I could not tell him, "You don't understand." I said, "I'll get back to you next week."

I called Lu Palmer; I called Reverend Evans and said we need to consider this boycott. They said, "You know, it's hard to do. We can't say no, because it's rational." So, by that Wednesday, about fifty-odd groups came together—Joe Gardner, a lot of people came together—many of whom had not been together for a long time. We decided we were going to give each other a chance. There was a sense of redemption in that meeting. A sense of, let's give each other a chance. No matter what side of the spectrum, in the machine, out of the machine, let's try it. And that Saturday morning at PUSH, we announced the ChicagoFest boycott. We then began to call the artists; people like Odetta said, "I will not cross your picket line." Stevie Wonder said, "I will not cross the picket line." When these big artists said they would not cross the picket line, that gave it added momentum.

We then had ten days of picketing in front of ChicagoFest, and really ten days of mass media access and education, because they measured each day whether or not the boycott was successful. That gave us a sense of focus, and we then said, let's take this to the next conclusion. Ed

Gardner of Soft Sheen Products financed a voter registration drive, and Lu Palmer had been arguing the case, "We'll see in '83; we'll see in '83."

Of the people who were considered for running, it was just a sense that Harold Washington was the best. Harold had been in the machine, but he had become an independent Democrat, so he knew forces on both sides. He had a sense of its internal mechanism. He had a sense of independence. Thus, he had credibility that made him a bridge builder, so to speak. Harold said, "I really don't want to run. I'm in Congress now. I finally have something I really want to do." He had become a good congressman rather quickly because he had the background as a legislator. He said, "I'll tell you what. If you really want me to run, register fifty thousand new voters and raise 200,000 dollars." That was his way of saying "I don't have to run."

Well, because the spirit was high, we registered nearly *four hundred* thousand voters, raised nearly a *half million* dollars. Harold could not say no, and thus, out of that context, the Harold Washington candidacy was born. It was the protest at the Chicago Housing Authority, it was the ChicagoFest boycott, it was the mass education, it was the voter registration. Harold said, "I have three demands. One, there must be one candidate: maximum unity in the base community, the African American community." He said, "But we can't stop there. There must be coalition. Reach out to the Hispanic community, to labor, and to progressive whites, because Chicago is a coalition city. We must find common ground across these lines of race, region, religion, and the ward, and thus that coalition was in fact the force that prevailed.

HAMPTON: [Richard G.] Hatcher told me that the Black middle class, too, was a significant factor. That they took the initiative after some reluctance at a certain point.

JACKSON: Well, I think it's fair to say that when you really make progress is when you rise above these class divisions, which become a way of putting people down. Who is the most loyal? Who is the Blackest? Who is the most dedicated? At some point in time, we must deal with our commonality, because our caste system, or our skin color, is more pronounced than our class system. As people like [Ralph] Metcalfe began to fight police brutality, for example, a dentist was beaten to death, and so it's your pedigree, not your class, that becomes the final factor. And when a community hits that point of dignity, and it fights insult with dignity, and finds common ground above skin color, and above religious denominations, and finds its commonality in its dignity, not division in its classes, you have a very powerful force.

HAMPTON: Tell me something about Harold Washington. From all I've seen and heard of him, he was a magnificent man. Give me some recollection, impressions of him.

JACKSON: You know, I shall never forget when, when Dr. King was leading marches in Chicago, there was the "machine" Blacks, the Silent Six, who could not protest because they were operating within the context of Daley's apparatus, and that was the independent struggle. Well, obviously the independent forces identified with Dr. King. The machine forces, the religious leaders, the political leaders, actually had a press conference. Some of them were singing songs to Daley, serenading Daley. "Must Daley bear the cross alone and all the world go free? Give us this day our Daley bread."

It was humiliating, you see, and so we had this division, a kind of class division, in the movement—not in the movement, in the machine. One day I was talking to Harold Washington and Rudy Polk in Harold's apartment right down from my office on Forty-Seventh Street. Harold gave me—it was a four-hour meeting—it was almost a tearful analysis of how he had grown up with the desire to be free, just like anybody else. Now he admired and respected Dr. King, but the Chicago political options were of such, there was some good people trapped in the machine and there were some not-so-good people not *in* the machine, some not in it because they couldn't get in it. It was more complex than with Dr. King or not with Dr. King, and he explained his evolution toward independence. He'd say, "He knows it, he studied it, and the precinct captain in it don't like it." This was 1966. This was, like, six years before he really made his public break with the machine.

Harold had a tremendous sense of etiology. Harold was an intellectual and a political activist, so when he became mayor, it was not just a ceremony. "Now, I am mayor." He said, "Now that really means reform government. It means open government. Open the books. Fair government, fair job distribution and promotions and contract distribution and ethical government." Well, in Chicago that's revolutionary government, you know? Open, fair, ethical government, where Chicago becomes our kind of town. He had a sense of etiology and a sense of political integrity. He was a man whose shoulders were as broad as Chicago's broad shoulders. He was tough enough to be equal to the task of being mayor of that city.

HAMPTON: You've just blown through about six of my questions. [*laughs*]

JACKSON: Moses got to the Red Sea and had a rod, and had a fit of faithlessness. He dropped the rod, and the blessing became a cursing, and could have bit him and destroyed him. It was not that he regained his faith in God that he picked up the rod and stretched out his hands. A people with a vote, with a broken spirit, will not pick it up and use it. Harold was able to renew our faith and bring about this broad-based coalition and people's minds and their votes and their sense of obligation, opportunity, and privilege consolidated in this man. He had this tremendous person, and within him we found a comfort and a security. And so, the miracle was unity in the community and reform government, *reform*. Open, fair, ethical, reform government. Maybe even for Chicago and maybe for the nation. Revolutionary government.

HAMPTON: Tell me the story about [Walter] Mondale coming to town.

JACKSON: In route to Harold's victory there was a sense, finally, that we could win. We didn't have the money. I mean, Byrne had the money, and Daley had the favor of many, and

Harold was a long shot. He didn't have the money, but he had the skill and the will to work. We were on a roll; we had momentum. We heard that Ted Kennedy was coming to town to support Jane Byrne, and Mondale was coming to town to support Daley. So, I called fifty leaders around the country. I got Willie Brown, and Maxine Waters, and congressional caucus members to appeal to them that they were for the liberal, progressive agenda. Here was Harold, a Democratic congressman. "Don't violate us in this way."

They said, "We have to come, because we made these commitments." There was a sense that we had been abandoned by liberals, that somehow liberators had to meet liberals, and if the most progressive liberals, Mondale and Kennedy, had this disregard for what the Chicago movement meant, we could only change that by becoming their peers. That meant someone had to begin to run against them in the primaries and function at their level of party politics.

Well, I began to raise the question that a Black ought to run. It was far from my mind, running, because if I had had politics on my mind, at that time, for myself, and Harold ran for mayor, I would have been considering running for his job as congressperson—but that was not really on my mind. I was still protesting to open the system up. I kept raising it, and of course it was met with a certain amount of contempt. "Aw, be serious, who can run? Who is qualified?"

I said, "Somebody should run."

I met with Andy Young three times. I tried to convince Andy to run. Andy'd just become mayor. He said, "I don't want to do it. I don't think it would work."

I said, "Andy, someone needs to do it." I met with

Maynard Jackson twice. Maynard was now out of politics. He was in the business. He was credible. He was articulate. He had all of the right stuff, and *he* wouldn't do it. I kept raising the proposition. It became a part of national debate: Should someone do it or should they not? At some point, "Run, Jesse, Run" began to emerge. I wanted to pull back but I couldn't because it would have appeared as if I had been insincere, that I was playing with the people. I was not playing, but I was not talking about myself. I had made almost no preparation to run, but then somebody had to run, so it is out of that context of fighting for Harold and fighting against liberal contempt that my own candidacy emerged out of this crucible, out of this process.

HAMPTON: Give me some feeling for Resurrection City. That was sort of like an early Rainbow experience. What was it like with all the different kinds of people?

JACKSON: The context of it is, the Saturday morning before Dr. King was assassinated, he called this emergency staff meeting at his office in Atlanta, Georgia. He had this vision that we should wipe out poverty, ignorance, and disease, but you couldn't do it on an ethnic basis. There was never going to be any plan to wipe out Black poverty that would leave the Hispanics in poverty, or whites, or women in poverty, or Native Americans in poverty. We had pull people together.

On this Saturday morning, he said, "I've had a migraine headache for three days. Sometimes, because our movement is divided, I feel like turning around, just quitting. Or maybe becoming president of Morehouse College."

Andy Young said, "Dr. King, don't talk that way. Don't say 'peace, peace,' when there is no peace.

"Let me finish," he said. "I can't turn around. People like [W. E. B.] Du Bois and Frederick Douglass and Mary McLeod Bethune, they wouldn't let me turn back. Then I thought about fasting, maybe to the point of death. Even though Stokely [Carmichael] and [H.] Rap [Brown] and [Jack]Whitten and Roy [Wilkins] may have different points of view on, on strategy, we're still friends. At the point of death they would come to my bedside, we could reunite." And then he said, as if something struck him, "But we will always be able to turn a minus into a plus. We can turn a stumbling block to a stepping stone. Sometimes my works feel to be in vain, but then the Holy Spirit comes; I'm revived again."

He preached himself out of a depression, so let us move on from there on to Memphis. He was killed on April the 4th. The struggle had to continue. We were going toward Resurrection City, Renewal City. Well, Dr. King was killed April 4th. Robert Kennedy killed June the 5th. There was a sense the White House had abandoned us and our leaders were dead, and I remember on this particular morning coming to Resurrection City, and Dr. Abernathy had appointed me mayor of Resurrection City. There I was, the mayor of a Washington city, not too far from the White House. I looked in the faces of the people, mostly women and children, and I had nothing to offer them, no money, and they had . . . no money even to get back home.

I remember having read a book by Dr. Howard Thurman, *Jesus and the Disinherited*, and he talked about when you're down to your irreducible essence and you have nothing, yes, no material thing, you have your person. You're still somebody. You're God's child. I said to them, "Repeat these words: Say 'I am.'"

They said, "I am . . ."

"Somebody. I may be poor, I may be unemployed, I may be unskilled, but I am somebody. Respect me. Protect me. Never neglect me." The whole "I am somebody" came out of that context in Resurrection City. The next day we had to march for some food. We decided to march to the Agriculture Department because we were putting focus on feeding and nutrition. We went and took a couple hundred people there, and we had been eating out of cans and the like down at Resurrection City—raining, in the mud, and good, good food in the Agriculture Department.

They were very nervous because we were there, and the cameras were there. I said, "Well we thank you very much."

They said, "But, who's going to pay us?"

I said, "I tell you what: You should submit us a bill between what you owe us and what we owe you. We'll pay the difference."

The guy said, "No, you're crazy. This is not the Agriculture Department, this is a private service."

I said, "We've come to the Agriculture Department to eat. Count up what you owe us and what we owe you." Dr. King had preached his 1963 speech about a balanced check. And so, we left. They wouldn't arrest all of us, but the next day they did make Dr. Abernathy force us to pay for the meal. [*laughs*] That was the context of that meal.

HAMPTON: What were your feelings when Resurrection City was closed down?

JACKSON: There was a sense of betrayal, a sense of abandonment. The dreamer had been killed in Memphis and there was an attempt now to kill the dream itself, which was to feed the hungry, which was to bring the people together, and rather than come forth with a plan to wipe out malnutrition, they were wiping out the malnourished. The first time I had ever really experienced tear gas was in Resurrection City. They drove us out with tear gas. They gassed us. They shot Dr. King, now they were gassing us. They didn't change the law, and after that period, no one else since that time has ever been able to set up any kind of a tent or protest arrangement there on those grounds. I was determined to keep the struggle moving, if you will, to keep hope alive, but I left there with an awful sense of betrayal and abandonment.

HAMPTON: How did you first learn about the police raid on Fred Hampton's apartment on the morning of December 4, 1969? What was your reaction?

JACKSON: Well, the news blasted out—there was a sense of intolerance toward the Panthers by the police, because they had this sense of agitation to bring clarity to what they call "exposing the contradiction." They would feed the children as a way of dramatizing the malnutrition. They would challenge police brutality which had become, in many ways, a way of life. And of course, they irritated the police, and there was this organized raid to kill them. For some time, there was an attempt to cover it up, but people like Dr. Charles Hurst wouldn't let it go. I remember Bobby Rush, who was Fred Hampton's closest friend, they went to kill him too, but he was not where they went to get him.

Bobby Rush was being sought, he felt, to be killed. They invaded the house where he was living. I received a call early in the morning, one Saturday morning, that he was a fugitive and he was going to turn himself in to me before the people on the platform at our regular Saturday morning Breadbasket meeting. By turning himself in to the police before several thousand people, that became his protection. I actually preached Fred Hampton's funeral and my sense was, in those first few days, the media was so anti-Panther, it was as if their being killed was a kind of relief. Then the community realized that blood had been spilled, an assassination and a massacre had taken place. From the point of Fred Hampton's blood to Harold Washington's inauguration, there's a kind of straight line of indignation and dignity fighting insult. So, Fred Hampton's assassination, and Mark Clark, is very much a part of the equation for changing the politics of Chicago.

HAMPTON: The Panthers used a great deal of profanity, like "off the pig," and threats. How'd you react to this?

JACKSON: I learned early on to separate their language from their message. It was their way of expressing a sense of violation, a sense of not being stakeholders, of being locked out, and though I had another language pattern, our message was the same. I'd just met with Fred, for example, and Bobby, a few days before he was assassinated, and had a sense of kinship with them. Of course, when he was killed, his parents asked me, as well as the other Panthers, to preach the funeral because I had a sense of him and his history and what he was about.

HAMPTON: One final question, not about the Panthers, about the Civil Rights Movement and us. What have we wrought? What has been the price that we've had to pay for what we've done with the Civil Rights Movement?

JACKSON: Well, we've started from further back than anybody else. After all, the Constitution designates African descendants as three-fifths human. No immigrant group had to face that mathematical equation. Three-fifths human? A little lower than people, a little higher than animals. Two hundred fifty years of free labor—just the interest from that, you know, would free us economically now—another hundred years of legal apartheid, the segregation in this country, and after all of this struggle, public accommodations, equal access, and protection under the law as opposed to "separate but equal," now the right to vote. I mean, the most fundamental shift from slave ship en route to championship has been to be empowered, to be enfranchised with this right to vote. I submit to you that in 1988, I got more votes than Mondale got for the nomination in 1984. Within our lifetime, this ongoing struggle will have an African American as nominee of a party, indeed, as president of the United States of America, and so the goal is within reach.

"YOU PLANT SEEDS THAT MAY BRING FORTH TREES UNDER WHOSE SHADE YOU MAY NEVER SIT"

INTERVIEW BY LADORIS CORDELL
COMMONWEALTH CLUB WORLD AFFAIRS OF CALIFORNIA
NOVEMBER 29, 2018

LADORIS CORDELL: Reverend Jackson: Frederick Douglass, Shirley Chisholm, and you were African American candidates for president from a major political party. Douglass received a single roll call vote at the 1888 Republican convention in Chicago, Chisholm sought the Democratic nomination in 1972 in Miami Beach, and you in your 1984 and 1988 presidential campaigns—now get this, folks—won a total of sixteen state contests and millions of votes, making you the first viable African American candidate for president. Now, when you ran there was no social media presence to speak of. Today, it's all about Facebook, Instagram, Twitter, and more. Compare, if you will, your experience running for the presidency in 1988 with what you observed in the 2016 presidential campaign. What's in store for us in 2020, and that race, and can things get any worse?

JESSE JACKSON: Things can get worse, but they need not. I was driven by a quest for personal dignity in public policy. In 1960, when I came home from college, I had to do a speech with twenty-five annotated bibliographies, and I went to the colored library and Mrs. Smith said, "We don't have this many books, but my friends at the Central Library will let you use her books."

So, I ran there, and she told me I had to wait seven days.

I said, "There's just two of us in the library."

She said, "Seven days."

The police said, "You heard what she said."

I went outside and I cried. I said, "This summer, I plan to use this library, and that was five years after Dr. King had emerged in Montgomery. Seven classmates were arrested that summer trying to use the public library, so that was a quest of personal dignity. Couldn't use the library in Greenville, South Carolina, couldn't use restaurants in Greensboro, North Carolina, and I couldn't vote. My father, a Second World War vet, had to sit behind Nazi POWs. *Dignity.*

As I learned what was happening and began to fight, these were matters of public policy. In '84 we thought we had the chance to win in Chicago, so we called the ChicagoFest boycott, because [Mayor] Jane Byrne had not been very kind to us.

In the middle of that thrust, we heard that [Walter] Mondale was coming to town to defeat us in the primary—Democrats, you know—so we sent them a telegram signed by Willie Brown and signed by Mrs. King and a number of us: "Please don't interfere with our will to become mayor of Chicago." Big deal after the '68 explosion there.

They said, "We have to come; our friends are there." Kennedy came for Jane Byrne, Mondale came for [Richard] Daley. I said somebody needs to challenge them in the primary. I asked Maynard Jackson, would he do it? And asked [Atlanta] Mayor Andy Young if he would do it. Andy was uniquely qualified. He had been Dr. King's right-hand person; he had been a congressperson, and a mayor. He wouldn't do it.

People started saying, "Run, Jesse, run!" It was a breakthrough. People were yearning for something, for somebody. So, we burst forth learning the process, and I learned even then there are certain timeless, changeless values in changing times. On the run for equal and adequate protection of the right to vote. That's a simple proposition. To free Mandela, which was at that time difficult because he was on America's terrorist list, but we argued for it. Let's talk Middle East policy as opposed to no-talk policy, and to stop drugs from coming in, jobs from going out.

We took several basic premises and we ran, and people began to respond. It was a glorious moment.

CORDELL: Amazing. So, what do you think's in store for us in 2020, just in terms of the rhetoric, the tenor.

JACKSON: We have more access to vehicles of communication, but we must drive the medium of what we say, not just be driven by what's available to us, and my sense is that if you use the media for life over death, healing and hope over hurt and hate, it's a good medium, but it can be used for the wrong reason. What happened on Facebook, for example. The last campaign was an attempt to challenge privacy rights, and that attempt was to troll and to in fact help determine the outcome of an election through that process. We must also put checks and balances on all this media.

I think, at the end of the day, whoever's running must

have the principles more of the moral center than left or right. I mean, left and right are two sides of the same coin that results in one party of two names. The moral center's to the left of that. In slavery times, the bad guys said treat them as you want to, good guys said be kind to them. Abolitionists said end that system, and to go beyond what the two systems were.

Today, there's no reason why we cannot have free public education for colleges. We're able to do that. That's a fight; it's the right fight. The idea of having babies locked up on the border is so disgraceful. To have the U.S. Army threatening to take border babies—Jesus was a border baby, if you will. It's morally disgraceful. The values that we need to argue for do not depend upon Facebook and Google and Microsoft, as it were. It depends upon the will of the leader to accept responsibility for putting forth a vision, and then make people better off.

CORDELL: So, it was 1968. Dr. King had been assassinated and Ralph Abernathy assumed the leadership of the Southern Christian Leadership Conference, SCLC. At that time, you were in charge of Operation Breadbasket, and that was an SCLC initiative to monitor companies' treatment of African Americans and to organize boycotts for fair hiring practices, but friction developed between you, the young upstart, and Abernathy, the establishment leader, such that you left to form Operation PUSH, People United to Serve Humanity. Now, fast-forward to 2018. We just completed the midterm elections in which the Democrats' blue wave took the House while the Republicans' red wall kept control of the Senate, and now there looms a fight on the Democrat side between self-described progressives—the young upstarts—and establishment Democrats over who will be the next speaker of the House. Talk to us about your experience as the upstart back in the day, and give us your view about the current situation among Democrats as they move to take charge of the House in January. Is this a case of Democrats misbehaving, or is it a case of Democrats behaving? Should the newbies challenge leadership, or should they shut up, listen, and learn from the elders? Or is there some in-between?

JACKSON: Should I leave now? [*audience laughs*] No, you know, actually the tension in part was because I was in Chicago, he was in Atlanta. Seven hundred miles apart. Some tensions developed and we formed an organization with the same people who threw us out of Chicago. We maintained a close personal relationship; it was not led to get ugly, because I was thinking about Mandela and his law partner back in 1946. They joined the ANC [African National Congress] youth movement. They built upon what was already there because why start from zero when I have shoulders on which you can build?

I would say to any younger generation, there's nothing new. Take the best of what exists and be transformative. For example, if the issue today is livable wages, if the issue is woman's right to self-determination, if the issue is less nuclear weapons, if the issue is to stop being draconian on our immigration policy: If those issues matter to you, you should build upon that. You need not start anew. That's why I think it's smart for Democrats to spend more time on issues that matter, that embrace all of us, than arguing about whether or not Nancy Pelosi should be there because of her age. Mandela came out [of prison] when he was seventy-two. It was direction, not age. If she were against Planned Parenthood, if she were against the protected right to vote, that's a legitimate argument. Arguing that she's seventy and you're forty because you can't be thirty-nine any longer. And you ain't forty-one yet. That's a bogus argument, because at the end of the day we must have one big tent where all are involved and none are locked out. If you build some argument for locking people out based on their age, they come right back in next time. "Vote for me, I support seniors." Support seniors, then.

Seniors can be leaders, yes. But often—Dr. King was twenty-six. He was a young leader. He came out of the NAACP. So, I am very much toward building upon that. I think Democrats, given the threats we are facing today, would do well to address what ails the people, and not just during midterms. For example, you see eleven Jewish people shot down in cold blood on a Saturday morning. First, they're talking about his hair blowing in the wind. You look at the people shot, and the president's response is, "Suppose the security guard had a gun." What can you do with a semiautomatic weapon and a gun if somebody is that sick and loaded with these weapons.

Look at Charlottesville, and you see equating civil rights protesters with these anti-Semitic racist Confederates, and you dismiss it. We need people to address those issues that matter. People need health care *now*. We need adequate education *now*. Jobs that pay *now*. Respect based upon their person, not based upon anything else. We're a multicultural, multi-educational society, a multiracial society. Those who embrace those values—if they're ten or eighty—embrace them because some young people don't make sense, and some do. Some old people don't make sense, and some do.

CORDELL: That's right.

JACKSON: You have to judge people based upon direction and vision, not based upon any other false premise.

CORDELL: Can I get an amen on that? [*crowd responds "amen"*] Reverend Jackson, in 2013, the conservative majority of the United States Supreme Court, in *Shelby County v. Holder*, gutted a key provision of the Voting Rights Act of 1965, and since then, several states have just come up with creative ways to suppress the vote. Interesting fact: Ninety-nine bills designed to suppress the votes of people of color were introduced last year, in thirty-one state legislatures. I was stunned, and I've been around a long time, but I was stunned by the blatant efforts to suppress the votes of Blacks, Latinos, and Native Americans in the midterms. How can America keep its promise to preserve our democracy if we can't be certain that our voices will be heard?

With so much at stake in the midterms, only 47 percent of eligible voters even bothered to cast their ballots, and that was a fifty-year high, so how do we get more people to vote? Should voting be regulated by the federal government rather than by the states? How do we do that? How do we ensure our votes?

JACKSON: You covered a lot of territory there. [*laughter*] Well, I think there should be a unified national voting process, not a states' rights vote, so that should be federal and unified. We have fifty states [with] separate and unequal elections on Election Day. In New York and Pennsylvania and Michigan, you can only vote one day, on Tuesday. In Georgia, you may have thirty days of preregistration. I mean, it's all over the place. As a matter of fact, in 2000, [Al] Gore was on the verge of beating [George W.] Bush and the Supreme Court intervened and gave the state the power to determine the winner. What they did was, they stopped the count with Bush ahead by 537 votes, but 27,000 votes, mostly black, had not been counted. The state determined the outcome of the election. I don't support states' rights on voting. You can't trust it. On the last election, Hillary Clinton won by three million votes. You have a one-person, one-vote democracy? You don't. Hillary Clinton won the election. Hillary Clinton won the election. Hillary Clinton won the election. It should've been another way.

I'm amazed at how many people, some that have this animus towards her, say, "If she had just done X or Y." Given the amount of international intervention and invasion in the process, given the amount of schemes and gerrymandering and undercutting, she had a three million surplus. Kennedy beat Nixon by 112,000 votes, less than one vote per precinct. Nixon beat Humphrey by 500,000 votes. She won by three million votes, so it takes effort to me to diminish what she did. If any of those had those odds, the odds of Russian intervention, the odds of manipulating Facebook, if any of them had those odds, none of them would have won, and so I think we would do well not to ever fall to the lie of diminishing what she did against the odds she did it against.

The other thing that happened during this season, in the darkest hours when it's real dark, the stars are most apparent. The gloom and doom around the kind of things that Trump had done and promised to do . . . when the election was lost, America didn't run and hide. We turned our pain to power. The pain we felt the night of November the 8th became a wake-up call as opposed to a go-to-sleep call.

So, Trump was installed, and one day, a million-plus women marched, and after those women marched, they went home and registered, voted, ran, and won. Part of what makes America great is the right to fight for the right, on a rather predictable time schedule. In the darkest hour, out comes some guy named Beto O'Rourke from Texas, who ran with the kind of strength and vigor and vitality and appearance that makes him high up for 2020 consideration. Who was he six months ago? Out of that dark season comes [Andrew] Gillum, in Florida—a black guy in Florida, yes—he ran a race. Each of those races pulled in a million new voters. And the race with Stacey Abrams in Georgia—who won the race, really. She was running against the secretary of state, who was the referee, scorekeeper, and timekeeper.

We have a Black woman lieutenant governor in Illinois, a Black-Jewish coalition [of Governor J.B. Pritzker and Lieutenant Governor Juliana Stratton]. In Virginia, in Michigan, in New Jersey, so in the darkness, I see the lights coming on everywhere, and it gives me inspiration for 2020.

CORDELL: One important way that America has kept its promise of freedom and equality for all is with an independent judiciary. The courts have been the salvation for women, the criminally accused, the poor, people of color. Groundbreaking decisions by the U.S. Supreme Court ended segregation of public schools, public accommodations, abolished the ban on interracial marriage, legalized same-sex marriage, and established procedural protections in our criminal justice system . . . we've always been able to rely on our courts when all else failed, but now the independence of our judiciary is being threatened by the Trump Administration, so much so that recently, Chief Justice Roberts made a rare public statement about the importance of preserving judicial independence.

There have been personal attacks against judges whose rulings this president disfavors, and there are a record number of federal judges whose qualifications are either suspect or whose judicial philosophies align with ultraconservative views, who've been confirmed to lifetime appointments on the federal courts. Now, my question to you is, with a U.S. Supreme Court majority that is solidly in the conservative camp, does all of this now mean that we can no longer turn to the courts for our salvation? How do we counter these unprecedented attacks on our courts?

JACKSON: We could not turn to the courts solely. The same court ruled blacks had no rights whites are bound to respect. We didn't give up then. That same court ruled in 1896—legal apartheid, legal segregation. That same court, against the odds, finally ruled in '54 apartheid was illegal. So, it's been a struggle against the courts through the years. The courts did not stop us from sitting in in 1955. The courts did not stop us from going to jail in 1964. It didn't stop us from marching in '65, and so I tend not to look for why we can't do it or why we must, it always starts by, as long as we have the right to fight for the right, nothing can stop us. No court will stop us.

Our quest for public accommodations . . . I look in the New South, when Alabama plays Georgia for the big game in Atlanta and there's [George] Wallace on the one hand saying, "I'll block the doors forever," and there's [Lester] Maddox with his ax handle saying blacks will never have the right to vote in the matter, and Dr. King about six blocks away, and these kids on the field: uniform color not skin color, direction not complexion, playing ball, the stands full of people, multiracial, multicultural. They could not stop that America. I think an America is coming forth for our future. Trump can turn back the clock; he can't turn back time. We're not going back. He's leaving, we are not.

The right to vote has been injured somewhat by removing preclearance, so much so . . . we got nine million more Democrats voted last week than Republicans, and yet we lost the Senate because of gerrymandering. When we got the right to vote in 1965, and I shall never forget, we thought, "We finally have the right to vote. The burden's on us to register." We didn't understand gerrymandering, annexation at large, roll purging . . . we didn't understand those manipulations. In '65, African Americans could not vote in the main in the South, white women couldn't serve on juries, eighteen-year-olds were serving in Vietnam but could not vote, you couldn't vote on college campuses, you couldn't vote bilingually, but we never stopped fighting, moving in the cracks. I say cracks advisedly because one morning I was walking down the street from my house and there was a broken sidewalk, and in the brokenness of sidewalks, some grass and flowers blossoming. I stop—I often stop in search for a sermon someplace. That cement was designed to suppress all the dirt under it, but there was a crack in it, and a little water and a little dirt and some sunshine . . . out of that crack came the stem and the flower and fermentation. The extent to which we have that will to survive against the odds, then nothing can stop us.

Dr. Howard Thurman did much of his layman ministry here in San Francisco. This was around when he was a youngster in Sanford, Florida, where Trayvon Martin was killed, that his feet had a kinship with the sand. He didn't have his shoes on so his feet could touch the sand, and this is Beech-Nut, this is Juicy Fruit, you could tell what the flavor of the chewing gum was. [*laughter*] His two older sisters would not let him grow up. He was tall, six feet, about 185 pounds, and while walking in the blackberry briar patch one day, a little green, two-inch snake jumped out, and they froze. He stood there, put his foot on the snake, and they pull up on him. He was, all of a sudden, their big brother. He could protect them; he could provide security for them. He kept his foot down on that two-inch snake, all 185 pounds of him. He finally felt a little throb under his foot and he kept pressing. He found his manhood, and he kept pressing, and then he raised his foot and the snake dashed in the bushes. Against the odds, on your back, if you maintain the drive to survive, when the doors open, shoot through it. That's what happened in the election last week. In spite of these schemes of disenfranchisement, we took the House back, and that means Nancy Pelosi now has a platform and a voice. And check and balance power, and subpoena power, and hope. So against tremendous odds, we must be odds busters and dream makers; we must be odds busters and dream makers to survive.

CORDELL: To change the subject a little bit, the strong coalition that existed into the 1970s between African Americans and Jews, a coalition that was in the forefront of the civil rights struggle of the sixties, no longer exists. When Louis Farrakhan uses anti-Semitic speech, I don't hear African American leaders denouncing him and his words. Rather, I hear things like, "Yeah, he says bad things about the Jews, *but* he stands up for black folks." Well, in my world, there's no "but" on that subject.

This year has marked a stunning uptick in incidents of anti-Semitism in this country, so my question to you: You've had your ups and downs with the Jewish community. Where do you stand on this subject today? Should we strive to rekindle that strong Black-Jewish coalition that once existed, and if so, how do we do that?

JACKSON: I think in many ways, it was never frayed as they made it out to be frayed. I mean, through all of the tough times, we supported Israel's right to exist for security; there were tensions around Israel's relationship with South Africa as we fought to free South Africa. We managed to handle that as well. You look at the votes in the U.S. Congress on labor and public education, we're essentially in the same place; on climate change we're in the same place.

I think sometimes we'll take a leaf and act as if it's a limb. That's fake news. I think we cannot afford to be apart. When you look at the nine people killed in the church in Charleston, eleven killed in the temple in Pittsburgh, that's a message that will not go away. Schwerner, Goodman, Chaney buried in the soil in Philadelphia, Mississippi, where Reagan stood and said, "We're back." Our relationship is profound and deep, and its kinship is nonnegotiable. We can't negotiate the Schwerner, Goodman, Chaney blood. We need to face the forces of radical racism and anti-Semitism, so in some sense we don't have anyplace to go. In some sense we have a false sense of security, but I tell you, unless we come together as brothers and sisters, or we die apart as fools. When we were marching together in Charlottesville, when Heather Heyer was killed, we marched together in '63, marched together in '65. When Willie Brown won in San Francisco, we were together. When Tom Bradley won in LA, we were together. When Maynard Jackson ran and won in Atlanta, and when David Dinkins won in New York. These coalitions that invariably bring us together don't get the kind of focus, as it were, as some one discordant voice. I cannot measure Jewish relations by the fact that when I opened my campaign, the very day I opened it, the Jewish Defense League carved a hog and put it on the doorsteps of where I lived. That's not Jewish people, that's an edge. But we must be more mature than that. It seems to me we cannot afford to allow leaves to become limbs in our struggle to survive.

CORDELL: A few years ago, you stirred up a hornet's nest in Silicon Valley's tech companies by insisting that they cough up their reports on racial, gender, and ethnic diversity in the workplaces. Then in April of this year, you and Rainbow PUSH Coalition sent an email to twenty-five large technology companies, including Google, Facebook, Tesla, and Oracle, calling on them to release information on their hiring practices, board diversity measures, and employee retention statistics, in addition to keeping their latest diversity data. Have they coughed it up, and are these companies helping to keep America's promise of equal opportunity?

JACKSON: Not nearly as much as they should. They are all stuck at the 2 percent level, for, for the most part. We began this drive in part by, between my copartner who is here in the greater Bay Area, Reverend Joe Bryant. One hundred eighty-seven board members are white men, thirty-six women, three Blacks, and one Latino. We began to challenge them on boards of directors. No shortage of talent, shortage of opportunity. When Ken [Chenault] joins Facebook, he had the most mature, the most capacity to serve, reliance to serve. To get Deborah Lee on the board of Twitter, Jim Bale, who used to be chief operating officer of Boeing, on the board of Apple, they brought something to the table as Jackie Robinson did to baseball, as [Bill] Russell did to basketball. There's no talent shortage; there's an opportunity shortage. So much for their being new—they're about fifteen years old—they're worse than General Motors, and Ford, and Chrysler. So, I can't make up age or religion. They're young and exclusionary in their policies, and they have a false comfort zone with other white people. Somehow, we are a multiracial, multicultural society, and when we come from that talent pool, good things come our way.

There are now about twenty African Americans on boards, and there are more Latinos on boards, more women on boards, because we made it a visible issue. The next step is more Blacks and women in the C-suites, operational stuff that takes place every day. They're in the professional services—lawyers, agents, and marketing—and that ultimately acts as the capital. You can have the best mind, and the best idea. Whites can still get more money on an idea than Blacks can get on collateral.

One of my nephews grew up in Oakland, has a Ph.D. in engineering and mechanics, came out of Stanford. All his classmates went straight to Silicon Valley; he went straight home. Same degree and higher grades, he now teaches at MIT. It would have been logical to have a place in Silicon Valley. It's not for him. What do Blacks and Latinos represent, and women represent? Market, money, talent, location. Racism and sexism are unscientific, immoral, and limiting. There's no scientific basis for saying a woman has less capacity to fly a plane than a man. Women will pick up a plane and run it across the mountains on their back. Women can fly planes and can be surgeons. There's nothing any of us cannot do with something called opportunity.

Why are we so good at football? When you look at, say, the Warriors. If the Giants play the 49ers, why are there 80 percent black players on both sides of the ball? What about those sports areas—football, basketball, baseball, track—that make us so successful? Whenever the playing field is even, rules are public, rules are clear, referees are fair, and the score is transparent, we can make it. When the playing field is uneven, if Blacks have to run twelve yards for a first down and whites have to run eight yards (and they inherited some yards), that wouldn't work either. In those areas of life, where *rules* are just, we have better outcomes, but when you put inheritance over effort . . . Effort and excellence means a lot; inheritance and access means more. I say, effort and excellence and hard work means a lot, inheritance and access means *more.* Next year it will be four hundred years since African Americans have been in this country, four hundredth anniversary next year. Two hundred forty-six years in slavery, woke up one day free but not equal, with no compensation for 246 years of work without wages. We were assets in slavery, then became threats with the right to vote. Five thousand lynchings, led by the previous slave masters, without protection under the law. How do we go to from that and when Dr. King was killed in Memphis, to the White House, and Barack as president? Against those odds, we're still transforming America.

It seems to me it's that hope, and that belief in the future against all odds, that makes us great. You cannot figure out a way to survive, a way to succeed, unless you maintain the power of hope.

CORDELL: I'm going to give you a number. The number is forty-six. That's the number of American hostages whose freedom *you* have secured. Forty-six. Just for a quick recap, in 1983, you traveled to Syria to secure the release of a captured American pilot, Navy Lieutenant Robert Goodman. In June

1984, you negotiated the release of twenty-two Americans held in Cuba. On the eve of the 1991 Persian Gulf War, you traveled to Iraq, met Saddam Hussein, and secured the release of twenty Americans. And in April 1999, during the Kosovo War, you traveled to Belgrade to negotiate the release of the U.S. POW captured on the Macedonian border while patrolling with the UN peacekeeping unit.

My first question to you: Why did you do that, and secondly, what is your secret? How do you do that?

JACKSON: I have one unfulfilled ambition.

CORDELL: What's that?

JACKSON: If I could go to Washington and save America from Trump. [*audience laughs*] No, I think that by . . . First of all, I think leaders must see the world through a door, not through a keyhole. So often, we see the world through that door, and we see limited, we think limited, and we act in limited ways. Somehow, it is a door through which we see the globe, not just a map. What I've found in working is that there is a significant part of the world that . . . half of all human beings is Asian, half of them are Chinese . . . one of them is African, one of them is Nigerian, two-thirds of our neighbors next door speak Spanish. English is a minority language in our hemisphere. The Indians and the Americans and Russians combined. In that world most people are yellow, brown, black, Christian, poor, non-white, young, and don't speak English. In that world, every time I stepped outside of my world, to what then was called nonaligned nations, I believed that if I could get to Saddam Hussain . . . I could convince him it was more to his advantage to let them go than to keep them, and so we were able to convince him. But, when I was in Iraq, Syria, Yugoslavia, Africa, whenever we found a country where most people were poor, we underestimated the impact of religious leadership in that country, and intelligence deficits, and by arrogance pushed them away. They were really open, looking for something. I tried to provide that something; a bridge to America. I should never forget, Reagan had said, "Don't go to Syria because you can't get him, you don't know what you're doing, you may get somebody hurt. But if you do go, 'cause you have the right to go, bring him back." [*interviewer and audience laugh*]

I said, "I'll take that deal." So, we were able to convince [Bashar al-] Assad, finally, to let him go, and we brought him back, and Reagan had a big White House reception. His full cabinet was there.

Three things stood out in my mind. When we finally convinced Assad after three days to let him go, Assad said, "Reverend Jackson, I'll let him go, but I have to go through my cabinet. It's Christmas time, and they are all over Europe on vacation."

I said, "If I had one lawyer, it would be you. Mister lawyer, let my guy go." He did.

The second thing I remember, I was waiting for the press to ask me some profound question about foreign policy. We had thought it through. I had the sense that if I had foreign policy built upon international law, human rights, self-determination, economic justice, and shared security, those principles are binding principles, and so I had a sense of what to do. And personality plays a role in convincing people. The press asked me, "Reverend Jackson, who paid the hotel bill?" [*audience laughs*]

I got no credit for thinking. We do these things ten different times, you know? We never thought, "Oh, we were lucky."

The last point was, it seems to me we brought him back to the White House. President Reagan said, "Well, Reverend Jackson, I'll tell you, you can't argue with success. Congratulations!"

I said, "Thank you, sir." He's sitting down. I said, "What can I do for you, sir?"

He said, "Well, what did you do different from what my guys had done?"

I said, "First, I tried." [*audience laughs*]

He said, "Now, what can I do for you?"

I said, "What you can do for me is call Assad and say thank you." I'm not asking for money, or a grant. We had a no-talk policy with Syria at the time, and he asked me in a very big room. He called Assad. They talked and never stopped talking. Talking matters. Talk, talk, talk, then shoot, shoot, shoot. They talked, and they were kind of embarrassed not to talk to each other. Assad was happy because he was recognized by America for releasing a soldier; Reagan was happy his guy was back home. They found it was mutually beneficial and built upon that.

The key to any good negotiation is finding out what's mutually beneficial to both parties involved. That's why the climate agreement in Paris was so significant. Everybody had a common interest, and the whole world saw it—except today's commander—but the whole world saw the value in having a climate agreement in Paris, which we must now restore.

CORDELL: Absolutely. Would you have liked to have been an ambassador, and if so, to what country?

JACKSON: No. I had the opportunity to be ambassador to South Africa at some point, but I wanted to keep one foot closer to government and one foot out to be a change agent. I didn't want to be in a position where the Government could fire me. I said, with all due respect to our government, I just wanted the freedom to move, and to be supportive of our government on its best days and challenge it on its worst days. At my age, now, would I take that position? Under another president, yes, but not now. I find myself disagreeing with my president too much. I couldn't. I'd be fired the first month. [*audience laughs*]

CORDELL: Let's change up the pace. I want to do a lightning round.

A lot of Democrats are already making noise about running for president in 2020, and on the Republican side, Trump seems right now to have no apparent challengers. I'm going to give you the names of possible Democratic contenders, and I want you to give them a grade—A, B, C, D, or F—for how each, if elected president, would keep America's promise to preserve our democratic institutions and bring us together.

JACKSON: Not fair, but go on. [*audience laughs*]

CORDELL: Kamala Harris.

JACKSON: High grade. She has the integrity, the experience, and the touch to get the high marks. To be state attorney general of California, U.S. senator from California, and an African American woman, she's conquered enough odds with grace to get high grades.

CORDELL: Elizabeth Warren.

JACKSON: Double A. We have a consumer protection agency now because of Elizabeth Warren. They refused to recognize the department, so she got mad and became a U.S. senator. She has all the right stuff. She chose not to run against Hillary—which was a choice—but there's nothing in government . . . the Government is determined by vision, and she has a great vision. I give her high praise.

CORDELL: All right, he said he's thinking about running: Kanye West. [*audience laughs*]

JACKSON: As an entertainer, A.

CORDELL: As an entertainer, an A?

JACKSON: That's what he does. I respect that. Each of us must try to stay in our lane. [*audience laughs*] I have high regard for him. Last time he met with Trump he went to his thing. He came back a few days later and said he felt he had been used. He didn't like it. That's a good thing.

CORDELL: Bernie Sanders.

JACKSON: High grades. I really think that Bernie has the vision. I think there's a generation just beneath Bernie, with Cory Booker and Kamala Harris and Beto O'Rourke. I think there's a generation that's coming now that we must lend our shoulders and our support.

CORDELL: A couple other people have thrown their names out. Michael Avenatti.

JACKSON: I. [audience laughs]

CORDELL: Cory Booker?

JACKSON: A. Stanford football player, good grades, very articulate, very driven—

CORDELL: Rhodes scholar.

JACKSON: —Rhodes scholar, and all that, so he has the right stuff.

CORDELL: Maxine Waters.

JACKSON: [*holds up his fist in solidarity as audience cheers and claps*] Maxine speaks the most truth to power; she might not make it through the primaries. [*audience laughs*] What Maxine is going to do, in her lane, she is going to become chair of the finance committee. Banking and finance and Wall

Street are already trying to adjust to the storm that's coming. Sometimes a good coach looks at players and the coaches judge by where they fit, what they do well. Sometimes, when people are as audacious as Maxine is, they might not fit here, they might fit there better. What she does as an advocate . . . most congresspeople find a place in the Congress. She found a space outside of it, and I hope that she maintains the courage it takes to maintain that space, because that space is difficult to occupy. If you're on the committee, you vote on the silent committee, you have lots of protection. Maxine will go out on the wing and fly by herself against the headwinds.

I have the highest respect for Maxine. There is nothing she can't do—including be a good president, I might add; the bar has been lowered so low—but I judge her high as a leader. Leaders, at their best, don't follow opinion polls. They mold opinions. She's an opinion molder. That makes her different.

CORDELL: Okay, last one. You. [*audience laughs*]

JACKSON: I did my best on my best day. [*applause*] You know, a couple things on that: I think I made a contribution in that lane. In '84 we got three-and-a-half million voters and four hundred delegates, and that seemed off. I get 48 percent, you get forty-nine, and you take one hundred, which would undercut the spirit of my forty-eight. I said, this is not right. It was winner take all.

In '88 we got seven million votes and twelve hundred delegates. I got 48 percent of the vote, and I got that many delegates. It's called proportionality. That seemed like it didn't matter much, but in 2008, twenty years later, when Barack ran against Hillary, what struck me the most about Barack as a younger person, from my children's generation, he said one day he was watching us debate at Columbia against [Walter] Mondale and [Gary] Hart. He said as a student, that I didn't really make much sense to him and at that time, but this thing can happen. That's one of the gratifying features, that you plant seeds that may bring forth trees under whose shade you may never sit. I find joy in that.

Beyond that, in 2008, when he ran, (against the odds) Hillary won California, barely. Texas, Ohio, and Pennsylvania . . . under the '84 rules, she would have been the nominee. That's democracy. [Obama] didn't win California, but he kept his share of delegates. The '88 rules evened the playing field for him. I saw the joy of that, and I think that he did so well. I must say that. You have to judge him not just by his running ability, but by how tough the headwinds were. He lost a lot of state legislatures because people ran against race and never called it race.

There's a lot of stuff that made us lose ground when Barack was president. When he came into office, we'd lost eight thousand jobs the month before. A net gain of jobs every month for eight years, some more, some less. He came in office, twenty-six million Americans had health care, most of them for the first time, and they were so devious until they called health care Obamacare. They put a label on it that they guessed to be poison, and I met some women in Kentucky. They really wanted affordable health care, but they didn't want Obamacare! They didn't want the eggs. They were all confused.

Then he renewed connection with Cuba in our

hemisphere. He was able to make a loan to bail out all the automotive industry. The climate change, the environment law in Paris. Tremendous contribution, no hint of scandal. The dignity of his family alone was worth the investment in Barack. [*applause*] I think about his mother-in-law, raising those two daughters in the big house, reminds me of Moses raising him inside Pharaoh's house. To watch the dignity of those girls, watch Michelle, who, along with my daughter, grew up together in Chicago, and to watch him do so well against such odds, he makes my heart rejoice.

CORDELL: That's right. All of us. [*applause*] We have time for a few questions from the audience. Reverend Jackson, you've been a powerful advocate for ending racism in the criminal justice system, and for ending the death penalty. Do you have any counsel for Governor Brown as he ends his tenure, for Governor Newsom as he begins his governorship.

JACKSON: One thing you can do is look at state contracts. A fairer distribution of state contracts. Women and people of color, who may often need access to capital, on the inside track. That's a way to do it.

The other one is that many of our youth, in this scientific age, should be having, all over the state, youth tech summits. Our kids should learn apps, and codes, and programming in their formative years. That includes those who are in jail. So many in jail on nonviolent offenses. Use some of that idle time to learn. They can go from jail with a trade, to transportation, to a job, and reduce recidivism. I think there's no reason why we should be having to leave here and go to another country across the ocean—and I'm always supporting B1 children, because I think that we must keep our doors open—but you have potential right here in Oakland and San Francisco to get there. Our children can learn, will, and must. That has to be the foundation to it all.

CORDELL: Given your long-standing activism for decades, what strategy do you recommend for us, and people of good will, to combat the craziness of this country?

JACKSON: Part of what makes America great is the right to fight for the right, to know what its promise is. Its promise is a multiracial society. Multicultural. I mean, "France for the French, China for the Chinese, Japan for the Japanese . . ." America for your tired, your poor, your huddled masses yearning to breathe free. Something about that promise is America's uniqueness and greatness, because it is that sharing of ideas that makes all of us see the world differently, and see it in a bigger place. I would hope, in years to come, that we would know that.

I went to a high school yesterday, in Seattle. I asked students, "Do you have a basketball team?" And they scream, they have state champions the last two years. "Who's the captain?" The captain stood up." I said, "Captain, how many days do you guys practice?"

"Five, six."

I said, "What about Sunday?"

"Off on their own."

"That sounds like seven to me. Seven days of practice. How many hours a day?"

"Four . . . sometimes more."

I said, "You ever read when you're in practice?"

He looked at me like I'm crazy. "No."

"TV in practice?"

"No." He looked at me like I'm really crazy now. I said, "Can your girlfriend come to practice?"

"Oh, no, no, no."

I said, "Well then, if you sweat and you get real tired, are you gonna sit down? You can't sit down, and why can't you sit down? You've got to suck it up, keep running."

Since we're having a family meeting, I say, "Now, do you study six days a week?"

". . . no."

"Study two hours a night?"

"No."

So, I don't need any study on why if you're not careful, while your legs will run you in doors, your mind will not keep you, because you're not working on it. Against the odds, the poorest school in the state on demographics is the champion because of what their priorities are. Part of my sense is actually we're fighting to motivate them to excellence and to have uncompromising standards, and investment to make it happen.

CORDELL: If you were a twenty-five-year-old activist today, where would you spend your time and focus?

JACKSON: I don't know, in part because it's situation. You have to address life as you find it and deal with the cards on the table. I in part fought to use the public library because we were humiliated and couldn't use it. In part we fought to go to theaters because they were "colored only." In part I fought for the right to vote because my father came up in World War II, and Black and brown soldiers had to sit behind Nazi POWs on American military bases. I had to take it where I found it. This generation cannot make an impact on public accommodations; we have that. Right to vote: We must obviously remove the scheme *undermining* the right to vote, but your generation must fight to reduce nuclear weapons. That's your generation's fight at twenty-five.

Students should vote. Every eighteen-year-old should graduate with a diploma in one hand and a voting card in the other. There are more eighteen-year-olds than there are eighty-one-year-olds. Use that power. We didn't have the power fifty years ago. Students should vote on the campus where they attend school, not where they come from. If you're from San Francisco, or you're from New York, you should register to vote where you attend school, and impact where you are. That's how you maximize your power.

Our agenda's very much the same. How do we use social media today to communicate in ways we couldn't talk to each other many years ago? I'm a strong advocate of social media, but human beings must drive the message. The machine does not have the message. We must drive the message. We must use the machine, not be used by it.

THE LAST INTERVIEW: "TRUMP WANTS TO PULL US BACK INTO WHITE SUPREMACY"

INTERVIEW BY DAVID MASCIOTRA
THE NEW REPUBLIC
AUGUST 1, 2023

"I'm traumatized by the highs and lows of our struggle," the Reverend Jesse Jackson told me during a recent conversation in his Chicago home.

His wife of sixty-one years, Jacqueline, had prompted his confession with a critical assessment of the violence central to American history and the cultural inadequacies that inhibit political debate. "We often talk about 'wounded warriors,'" she said, "but we don't have the vocabulary to discuss those who served and who died in the domestic wars of our country—the wars to advance our country toward democracy."

"I had a protective Chicago police detail outside my home and office for thirty years," Jackson told me. The threat of death followed him no matter where he marched, spoke, or even slept. He watched his friend and mentor, Dr. Martin Luther King, die from an assassin's bullet to the neck. In the speech that King gave the night before his death, he reflected on his own mortality and the escalating hatred and menace he confronted on a daily basis, testifying that "longevity has its place"—but confessing that he did not expect to experience it.

While America is not yet the "promised land," it has undergone a profound transformation since King shared his mountaintop vision in 1968. Jackson played no small part in that progress. He has lived as a warrior and commanding general in many of the most critical battles for the realization of a multiracial democracy. He has enjoyed the very blessing that was so cruelly stolen from King, Malcolm X, Medgar Evers, and many other civil rights veterans: longevity. He is now eighty-one years old and the father of six children, one of whom, Representative Jonathan Jackson, was elected to Congress in 2022.

Jesse Jackson was diagnosed with Parkinson's disease in 2017. With challenges to his mobility and speech, he is stepping back at the Rainbow PUSH Coalition, the human rights and political advocacy organization he founded. At first, in the press announcement, he called it "retirement," but now he prefers the word "pivot." Frederick Haynes III, a Texas-based minister, was named the new president and CEO of the coalition.

Jackson's announcement comes at a time—the primary campaign season—when he twice made his mark on U.S. election history, with racially unprecedented and groundbreaking primary campaigns for president. So, he knows all about insurgent candidacies—and he is concerned at what he's seeing on the Democratic side today. He supports Biden's reelection but worries about the influence of Robert F. Kennedy, Jr. "He's wacky," Jackson said. "He's using the great legacy of his name to become Trump-lite."

His assessment of Cornel West, who is running for president on the Green Party ticket, is kinder: "He is a man of substance. He has a contribution to make to the dialogue, but he should do that within the party, not against it. In the 1980s, I won millions of votes and raised millions of dollars.

There were people who advised me to go third party. But I expanded the Democratic Party. I could have broken away, but I thought that would only help the right."

The Republican Party, Jackson suggests, has become too dangerous for such electoral distractions. "We'll win if we vote our numbers, but if we don't, we risk losing our democracy," he said. "Trump wants to pull us back into white supremacy. [Ron] DeSantis is even worse. He's a Harvard and Yale man. He knows better. There's something more insidious about that."

Spending time in discussion with Jackson doubles as a vivid tour of American history and engagement in the converging crises of the present. As he reflected on the triumphs and devastation he's experienced, he represented and articulated the ongoing urgency of America's long struggle for equality and justice. I detected worry that his life's work to help advance American democracy could be undone in an election or two.

The year was 1960. At home in Greenville, South Carolina, during a break in his first semester at North Carolina A&T University, he went to the "Black" library in town to check out a book he needed to write a term paper. The librarian told him that they didn't have it in their collection but assured him that her friend, a librarian at the "white" library, would break policy and allow him to take the book. At the larger, more modern library across town, he was attempting to check out the book when a police officer forcibly ejected him from the library and threw him down on the curb. Jackson told me that he sat and cried. But he later joined with seven other students to form what historians call the "Greenville Eight," which led an ultimately victorious movement to integrate library services in the city.

At North Carolina A&T, Jackson led protests against police brutality and organized with a local chapter of the Congress of Racial Equality, or CORE. In 1965, he interrupted his graduate studies at the University of Chicago to lead a delegation down to Alabama to participate in the Selma to Montgomery marches for voting rights. It was there that Jackson met Dr. Martin Luther King and earned a position on his staff. For the next half century, despite the risks and pain associated with civil rights activism, Jackson led efforts to integrate an apartheid economy. His fight against redlining, hiring discrimination, and exclusion of racial minorities from trade unions earned him the nickname the "apostle of economics." He led protests and boycotts against corporations like General Motors and Burger King and the giants of Silicon Valley, securing thousands of jobs for Black workers and millions of dollars of ancillary benefits for Black professionals and entrepreneurs.

In the 1980s, the Democratic Party was also in desperate need of reform. One might say that Jackson helped Democrats become "woke." When party leaders, including Senators Edward Kennedy and Walter Mondale, endorsed white opponents of Harold Washington in the Democratic primary for Chicago mayor in 1983, Jackson searched for a Black leader to run for president as a challenge to the "indifference and mediocrity of the white establishment within the party." When they all declined, Jackson himself ran. The mainstream press predicted Jackson would register as a mere asterisk in the 1984 race, but he defied expectations by winning nearly one out of every five votes. In 1988, he outperformed Joe Biden and Al Gore to take second place in the Democratic primary, ushering millions of new voters into the party. "We built a multiracial, multilingual, multigendered coalition," Jackson said to me, flashing a smile.

The Jackson coalition was also international. Uniquely successful in American history as an unofficial diplomat, he has negotiated the release of hostages and political prisoners in Syria, Cuba, Iraq, Serbia, Gambia, and Algeria.

Many political observers, including Steve Kornacki and Bernie Sanders, attribute Democratic control of the Senate during the Reagan years, and subsequent victories for Bill Clinton and Barack Obama, at least partially to new constituencies that Jackson brought to the party. He spoke directly to Latinos with Spanish translators, visited Asian immigrant neighborhoods in San Francisco and other cities, made campaign appearances on Native American reservations, and was the first presidential candidate to make gay rights central to his agenda.

Jackson's vision of a "Rainbow Coalition" was twenty years ahead of its time. "We prevailed in changing the Democratic Party's cultural power," he said. "Now we must build a movement for economic power." While he celebrates Democrats' leftward shift on economic policy, Jackson yearns for a popular social welfare movement similar in size and strength to the labor movement of the 1930s that encouraged President [Franklin] Roosevelt to enact the New Deal. As in the 1980s, Jackson today advocates for universal health care, tuition-free community and state colleges, paid family leave, subsidized childcare, raising the minimum wage to a living wage.

While much of what he's fought for remains a dream rather than reality, Jackson provided me with an appraisal of the quiet aspects of revolutionary change that many Americans now take for granted. "When Dr. King was leading us, there was only one Black elected official in the South," he said. "Now, there are Black mayors, Black congressmen and women, Black senators, Black city council members. And whites are voting for progressive Blacks. Hundreds of thousands of white people—in Georgia—voted for [Senator Raphael] Warnock."

Jackson pointed to the television, which was tuned to CNN. "We now have access to information," he said. "Black, Latino, progressive scholars and journalists appear on television, write for major papers, teach in academia. Dr. King fought against a very hostile national press."

When I asked what he considers his greatest achievement, he said, "We raised Black consciousness and enlarged the white conscience."

He then told a story from his 1984 campaign. An antagonist of big agriculture, he was scheduled to speak to family farmers in a rural area on the outskirts of Columbia, Missouri. When he and his staff arrived, they paused in horror to find an audience of white men in hoods. His fear quickly morphed into shock and relief when he learned that they had disguised their faces to prevent the Bureau of Farmers, which set farmer insurance rates, from identifying them as supporters of the Jackson campaign. (They worried the bureau would penalize them.)

"We went into hotbeds of white nationalism and Black nationalism," Jackson concluded, "from the fields of Iowa and Missouri to Harlem and the Black neighborhoods of Chicago and Detroit, and converted many people from nationalism to the rainbow."

Even if he will no longer work out of the Rainbow PUSH offices six days a week, as he did until recently, and even though [he] will spend more time seeing to his health, Jackson is not yet ready to truly retire. "I plan to teach seminars for seminarians and young ministers on how to fight injustice," he said. "I especially want to help Black and Latino ministers work together for social justice. We need to strive more toward a Black-brown alliance for social justice, because we're in the same fight."

I closed our conversation by asking Jackson about his personal battle with Parkinson's disease, which also afflicted his father. Every day, he says, people with Parkinson's write him to thank him for his example of perseverance. "I'm happy that I can inspire people," he said.

"I used to speak at middle schools and high schools," he added, "and I told them the same thing that I now tell people with Parkinson's." His words should guide anyone who still believes in the promise of American democracy, even as powerful forces gather to suffocate it: "You only drown if you stop kicking."

JESSE JACKSON was an American civil rights activist, politician, and Baptist minister. As a close friend of Dr. Martin Luther King, Jr., Jackson was instrumental in the Civil Rights Movement of the 1960s and '70s. He founded the Rainbow/PUSH Coalition and mounted historic campaigns for president of the United States in 1984 and 1988. He is widely regarded as one of the most consequential figures in the history of the Civil Rights Movement.

AL SHARPTON is a minister, activist, and one of the nation's most distinguished leaders in the fight against injustice. He has advocated for civil rights for over fifty years, since he was appointed by Jesse Jackson as youth director of Operation Breadbasket at the age of thirteen. Reverend Sharpton is the founder and president of the National Action Network, and hosts *PoliticsNation* on MS NOW as well as *Keepin' It Real*, a nationally syndicated radio show.

ARTHUR KRETCHMER was the editorial director of *Playboy* for more than thirty years. His writing has been published in the *Chicago Sun-Times*, *Newsweek*, and *The Village Voice*.

TONY BROWN is a journalist, newscaster, and founding dean of the Howard University School of Communications. His groundbreaking television show, *Tony Brown's Journal*, was the longest-running Black news program in television history, and the first on national television to cover the Untreated Syphilis Study at Tuskegee on Black men as well as the Tulsa Race Riot of 1921. He is the author of *Black Lies, White Lies: The Truth According to Tony Brown* and *Empower the People: Overthrow the Conspiracy That Is Stealing Your Money and Freedom.*

DIAHANN CARROLL (1935–2019) was an American actress, singer, and activist. She starred in the television series *Julia*, the first to feature a Black woman with a professional career, and was the first Black woman to win a Tony for Best Performance by a Leading Actress in a Musical.

RONALD SMOTHERS (1947–2026) was a journalist who spent forty years as a reporter for *The New York Times* and *The Washington Post*. He lectured at Harvard University's Joan Shorenstein Center, taught a seminar at Rutgers University, taught news writing as an adjunct professor at Brooklyn College, and was a Distinguished Journalist in Residence at the University of Delaware.

HENRY HAMPTON (1940–1998) was a filmmaker who founded Blackside, Inc., in 1968, three years after he participated in the Selma march in 1965. Blackside became the largest Black-owned film company from the mid-1970s until the late 1990s. Hampton produced over eighty programs, including *Eyes on the Prize* and *The Great Depression*. He received seven Emmys, an Academy Award nomination, and multiple Peabody Awards.

LADORIS HAZZARD CORDELL is a retired judge of the Superior Court of California and has devoted her career in the law to creating greater access and equal justice for people of color and low-income individuals. An author, artist, vocalist, and pianist, she resides in California with her partner and is the proud mother of two daughters.

DAVID MASCIOTRA is the author of six books, including *I Am Somebody: Why Jesse Jackson Matters* and *Mellencamp: American Troubadour*. As a journalist, political analyst, and art critic, he has written for *The New Republic*, *Salon*, *Progressive*, *Washington Monthly*, *No Depression*, *CounterPunch*, *CrimeReads*, and many other publications about politics, literature, and music.

THE LAST INTERVIEW SERIES

JIMMY CARTER:
THE LAST INTERVIEW

$19.99 / $26.99 CAN

978-1-68589-152-7
ebook: 978-1-68589-153-4

SINÉAD O'CONNOR:
THE LAST INTERVIEW

$19.99 / $26.99 CAN

978-1-68589-185-5
ebook: 978-1-68589-186-2

OCTAVIA E. BUTLER:
THE LAST INTERVIEW

$19.99 / $25.99 CAN

978-1-68589-105-3
ebook: 978-1-68589-106-0

bell hooks:
THE LAST INTERVIEW

$18.99 / $24.99 CAN

978-1-68589-079-7
ebook: 978-1-68589-080-3

KURT COBAIN:
THE LAST INTERVIEW

$17.99 / $23.99 CAN

978-1-68589-009-4
ebook: 978-1-68589-010-0

DIEGO MARADONA:
THE LAST INTERVIEW

$17.99 / $23.99 CAN

978-1-61219-973-3
ebook: 978-1-61219-974-0

JOAN DIDION:
THE LAST INTERVIEW

$17.99 / $23.99 CAN

978-1-68589-011-7
ebook: 978-1-68589-012-4

JANET MALCOLM:
THE LAST INTERVIEW

$17.99 / $23.99 CAN

978-1-61219-968-9
ebook: 978-1-68589-012-4

THE LAST INTERVIEW SERIES

JOHN LEWIS:
THE LAST INTERVIEW

$16.99 / $22.99 CAN

978-1-61219-962-7
ebook: 978-1-61219-963-4

FRIDA KAHLO:
THE LAST INTERVIEW

$16.99 / $22.99 CAN

978-1-61219-875-0
ebook: 978-1-61219-876-7

FRED ROGERS:
THE LAST INTERVIEW

$16.99 / $21.99 CAN

978-1-61219-895-8
ebook: 978-1-61219-896-5

TONI MORRISON:
THE LAST INTERVIEW

$16.99 / $22.99 CAN

978-1-61219-873-6
ebook: 978-1-61219-874-3

SHIRLEY CHISHOLM:
THE LAST INTERVIEW

$16.99 / $22.99 CAN

978-1-61219-897-2
ebook: 978-1-61219-898-9

GRAHAM GREENE:
THE LAST INTERVIEW

$16.99 / $22.99 CAN

978-1-61219-814-9
ebook: 978-1-61219-815-6

RUTH BADER GINSBURG:
THE LAST INTERVIEW

$17.99 / $23.99 CAN

978-1-61219-919-1
ebook: 978-1-61219-920-7

URSULA K. LE GUIN:
THE LAST INTERVIEW

$16.99 / $21.99 CAN

978-1-61219-779-1
ebook: 978-1-61219-780-7